From IRRELEVANT *to* INDISPENSABLE!

*How the Greatest Financial Advisers of
Our Time Use the Spoken Word to Leverage
Technology and Make it Their Greatest Ally*

RAO GARUDA

and

GARY SCHULTE

with GEORGE THOM

ARCHWAY
PUBLISHING

Archway Publishing books may be ordered through booksellers or by contacting:

Archway Publishing
1663 Liberty Drive
Bloomington, IN 47403
www.archwaypublishing.com
1 (888) 242-5904

Because of the dynamic nature of the Internet, any web addresses or links contained in this book may have changed since publication and may no longer be valid. The views expressed in this work are solely those of the author and do not necessarily reflect the views of the publisher, and the publisher hereby disclaims any responsibility for them.

Any people depicted in stock imagery provided by Getty Images are models, and such images are being used for illustrative purposes only. Certain stock imagery © Getty Images.

ISBN: 978-1-4808-7159-5 (sc)
ISBN: 978-1-4808-7160-1 (hc)
ISBN: 978-1-4808-7161-8 (e)

Library of Congress Control Number: 2018966755

Print information available on the last page.

Archway Publishing rev. date: 01/15/2019

About the Authors

Rao Garuda, ChFC, CLU, is a true American success story. Having arrived in the United States from his native India with just seven dollars in his pocket, he has become an iconic financial adviser, mentor, coach, and philanthropist. Professionally, Rao is consistently in the top one-tenth of 1 percent of all life insurance salespeople worldwide.

Rao's specialty is tax-advantaged strategies that use life insurance and other investments to offer clients the security of our best financial institutions, combined with his time-tested and innovative concepts. A highly sought-after speaker throughout the financial services world, Rao is best known for his wisdom, his mentoring, and his insights into the true value of his work on behalf of his thousands of clients.

Rao's charity goes far beyond his generosity toward his fellow financial service professionals. He has donated over $1 million to his favorite charity, providing clean drinking water to poor villages in his native India.

Rao routinely engages several of his doctor clients to accompany him to India to do pro bono work, providing prosthetic limbs to hundreds of disabled individuals.

Gary Schulte, CLU, has been called a "distribution alchemist." With more than fifty years of experience in designing, building, and managing product delivery systems at the most senior level of the life insurance industry, this veteran sales executive blends lessons of the past with his view of your future.

Gary started his field career as an agent, moving on to sales manager and finally becoming agency builder, eventually building his company's leading agency. He then spent twelve years as a chief marketing officer and life insurance company president. During this time, he directly oversaw some of the industry's most innovative products, strategies, and distribution channels.

Gary's consulting firm, Distribution Solutions, has been retained by several of the top ten life insurance companies, as well as by major banks and wire houses to assist with their product, marketing, and corporate strategies.

The author of three other books on financial services, Gary combines the unique experience as one of our industry's longest-tenured financial advisers and most noteworthy track records with his commitment to pass his lessons on to students and members of the Financial Services Network (FSN).

George Thom, ChFC, CLU, is the creator of the Decision Process software, the engine that supports the FSN Client Acquisition Process, which is a major theme of this book. George was recruited into our industry by his lifelong friend Gary Schulte. After becoming a member of Million Dollar Round Table (MDRT), he went on to become his company's number one agent while still in his twenties. But this was only preparation for his unique ability!

George is a mathematician and programmer, for which he is recognized as a genius. He converts the vision of Gary and the know-how of Rao into objective formats that allow clients to make informed decisions. George's creative approach to illustrating financial strategies has the *human touch that only a producer at heart could deliver.*

Brad Etheridge has been a driving force behind the creation, growth, and management of FSN. He is a valued mentor and coach and a sought-after joint work aficionado of our membership.

Brad is a master of discovery in two of the most important markets to our industry: doctors and business owners. He has conducted hundreds of doctor seminars and trained scores of advisers to do the same. His innovative approach to discovery in the business owner market has been Brad's trademark at FSN. Brad was generous enough to share some of his techniques with us. These appear in Chapter 4.

We also thank Jerry Vanderzanden, ChFC, CLU, for his astute and timely observations provided in Chapter 11. Jerry's views on the regulatory trends and sales practices are reflected throughout this guide and eloquently expressed in Chapter 11. We know of no field professional who understands the regulatory landscape from the perspective of an adviser better than Jerry.

I don't believe I'm going to teach you anything you don't already know.

I do believe you will be better off if you knew that you knew it!

—Werner Erhard, founder of est

This book is dedicated to those commodity-resistant financial service professionals who show promise for becoming indispensable.

CONTENTS

Authors' Notes

THIS GUIDE is a textbook for those who share the authors' beliefs about the indispensable value of the financial services professional.

Our students come from all corners of the financial services industry.

The Financial Services Network (FSN) was created to educate, train, and mentor financial service professionals (FSP) of various orientations. Our long-term goal is to help our students live up to their chief responsibility: helping clients make informed decisions about their financial future.

Our mission is to provide a forum for FSPs that will combine the voice of experience and cutting-edge technology with the chemistry that occurs when an eclectic group of established professionals gather.

The glue of our network is our faculty, which consists of the industry's leading financial professionals, marketers, and mentors, along with creators of the most innovative strategies.

Our sales training centers around the FSN Client Acquisition Process (CAP), which provides our path to achieving indispensability—a path that can lead some of our students to advanced markets. For others, it will simply codify their position in their existing market. For all, it will provide the key to avoiding irrelevance by using technology as a tool to make the FSP indispensable to clients!

We take three literary liberties in this guide, which we feel are necessary to place proper emphasis on key areas that will maximize value to the reader.

First, we attempt to isolate important statements by using *one-sentence paragraphs* throughout.

Second, we use a lot of *italics* for words and sentences to ensure they stand out.

Third, we could not tell this story of our profession, either historically or prospectively, without *multiple comparisons to doctors*. Physicians across the United States have been our clients, teachers, and friends. We hope the medical profession considers our references to them to be a compliment!

These three patterns are all a product of two of our dearest mentors, Jack and Garry Kinder, who were passionate about teaching us the importance of *overcommunicating*!

We trust the reader will not mind our repetition of core values, beliefs, and practices.

Financial Services Network
www.fsnprocess.com
800.997.5282

INTRODUCTION

THIS BOOK was written for a specific audience—the financial services professional (FSP) who will succeed and flourish with or without this book, with or without our mentoring, with or without sweeping industry changes, and even with or without commission-based products. This book is for someone we call *the commodity-resistant financial services professional*.

A book for those who don't seem to need it? Reread the dedication for a clue.

We're not angling for a big readership, just those FSPs who are adaptable, who are coachable, and who have an eye on the changing landscape of financial selling, especially those who may have a view of their own they may want to share as part of our curriculum at Financial Services Network (FSN).

We may have some important answers to the issues of the day, but we know from experience that the kind of students we attract make a significant contribution. That's why we are building FSN around a contributing *faculty of successors* who share the core values evidenced in this book. We have a lot of answers, but we know our faculty and students will contribute many more.

In the interest of full disclosure, we have a commercial purpose beyond this book. It is guide to a different style of selling, a style that, to be mastered, requires a lot more than just one reading, even with the use of a highlighter.

Our clearly stated intent is to introduce qualified advisers to the Financial Services Network.

We hope readers who agree with our views will invest a few days in one or more of our training events under the tutelage and guidance of our faculty. Those who qualify may want to take the next step and become members of our network.

We are confident that those who do neither will still benefit from this book.

That's not just a sales pitch. It's an offer from four seasoned and decorated *sales* veterans with collective experience of over 175 years.

Do the math. We won't be passing your way again!

The reader should also be alerted to the fact that this is a book about selling.

We make no apologies. On the contrary, we haven't seen a good book that was up front about the profession of selling in thirty years.

Our industry has created a litany of euphemisms for the term *salesperson*. The farther we get from our roots, the more troubling it seems to us.

Not presenting ourselves as salespeople has contributed to a disconnect between the rendering of advice, which is a commodity, and the instigating of programs of change for the better in a client's life, which is a valued service—a service that begins with the FSP being in charge and that, if properly executed, concludes with the prospects being fully engaged and inviting us into their lives.

That statement includes *all* financial service professionals.

This book is a guide (and we will refer to it as a *guide* going forward) for a sales process that will help readers deliver *a superior value to exceptional prospects.*

If FSPs follow our process, they will continue to receive the *greater-than-average* compensation they deserve, be it commission or fee based. That is going to take a lot of study, a lot of work, and dedication to deliver a better product to prospects and clients. It will also require coachability and a wiliness to adapt.

There was a time when the platforms from which the FSP operated offered an abundance of training, education, and mentoring and coaching on the basics needed for individuals to earn professional status within our industry.

Ironically, at a time when those things are more important than ever, the industry has all but abandoned these traditional basic tenants of successful selling.

> *Instead, the institutions, operating platforms, and product providers pour every available resource for education and development into the governance of market conduct and cautionary measures to protect consumers and themselves.*

Mind you, like most tightening of business practices and behaviors, these restraints were well earned—and not just by those who didn't get the job done right because of carelessness or incompetence.

It took more than incompetence to bring about the current level of oversight we are experiencing in our business. It required great cleverness and almost unfathomable greed to usher in the level of regulatory intervention we are now experiencing. As always, it took only a handful who knew how to use the trust of others as a weapon against them.

Amid considerable uneasiness about the current and future environment, we believe *our profession is on the cusp of an exciting new epoch.*

Recent developments in the economy and changes in the tax law have made the markets discussed in this guide the most target-rich in memorable history. And our memories go back a long way!

There has never been a more robust climate for serving the affluent, successful business owners, self-employed professionals, and anyone else who values expert counsel and is accepting of the cost associated with it.

To take advantage of the opportunity we see, *advisers from all corners of financial services* are going to need some solid education on the strategies that current tax law has made available. They also will need specialized training on how to sell themselves and their services under some of the new rules—all in a way that minimizes the risk of the prospect trying to "do this at home" and, most likely, making uninformed decisions by relying too much on technology.

We have a blockbuster answer for that issue too!

The only thing holding the established adviser back is his or her ability to adapt to the changing terms of engagement. We offer readers a strategy for three things:

First, a sales process that is client-centric and delivers value that cannot easily be accessed elsewhere by the prospect.

Second, a software system that enables advisers to offer objective choices to clients that eliminate conflicts of interest while supporting ethical standards.

Third, a network of like-thinking financial service professionals educated and trained in the ways of the future by willing mentors and faculty who are among the last of a storied generation in our industry.

PART 1

THE FIVE GREAT
RULES OF SELLING

Note: Following are three terms key to our system:

A **financial service professional (FSP)** is anyone who makes their living by offering financial products, counsel, coaching, planning, protection, service, accounting, or legal advice to the public.

The **Financial Services Network (FSN)** is a membership organization devoted to the education, training, and professional development of financial service professionals.

The **Client Acquisition Process (CAP)** is a proven selling system that combines mastery of the language of selling with the art of discovery and uses innovative software that empowers clients to make informed decisions.

(1)

A Brief History of
Our Beginnings

People without knowledge of their history, origin and culture are like a tree without roots.

—Marcus Garvey

EVERYONE KNOWS that it's impossible to trace the origins of humans selling things to one another. If we want to omit the human element, we could even make an argument that it all started in the Garden of Eden, when the serpent sold Eve on biting the apple.

For our purposes, we would rather identify a time when capitalism intersected with entrepreneurism, marking this as the beginning of salesmanship. We believe that seminal moment in the history of selling occurred in medieval times.

In those days, all produce, and other perishables were brought from the farms to the central markets inside the city walls. Since most of the feudal lords' subjects lived outside of the city walls, the journey to market by oxcart, or whatever, was quite daunting. Most had neither the time nor the resources to make frequent trips. Yet if they bought larger supplies of most anything, it would likely spoil before being consumed.

What's a peasant to do?

Enter some of capitalism's earliest salespeople. Some of those living a long way from the city walls decided to go ahead and purchase quantities of perishables far exceeding their needs.

Then, during the long journey home, as they passed others on their way to the market, these people would offer to sell some of their surplus merchandise to those they passed. These "customers" quickly learned that this practice saved them a load of time.

Of course, our pioneer salesmen could charge an appropriate premium over the "wholesale" price they had paid many miles back.

Eventually, these enterprising individuals would head to the gates of the city with larger and larger wagons. They'd pick a clearing between the outlying "suburbs" and put up their food stands. For their clever practice of grossing up the price of goods in exchange for convenience, they were eventually referred to by their customers as "grossers," and their venue was known as "the grocery."

The rest, as they say …

Every good book on selling usually has its own proprietary definition of the difference between marketing and selling. The foregoing story is as good a place as any for us to share our view. These individuals started as salespeople, selling goods to the others they passed on their way back home. Later, when they set up a location and began to get repeat customers, they evolved into marketers. This makes an important point.

Marketing generally refers to activities that help salespeople improve their performance. Although there are different definitions of both marketing and sales, it remains as simple today as it was for marketing pioneers.

We define *marketing* as everything you do to get in front

of a prospect. *Selling* is defined as everything you do, once in front of them, to convert prospects into satisfied customers.

Although most of us try to keep it that simple, the line between the two is becoming increasingly blurred today. As we shall see, the dynamics have changed because of automated marketing and electronic selling. That's a large part of what this guide is about.

We've all heard the admonition that "those who fail to learn from history are condemned to repeat it." In the coming chapters we're going to make sure you learn to do just that. But we aren't going to throw the proverbial baby out with the bathwater.

We're going to review the conditions leading to the evolution of sales practices that allowed sales people to triumph in the second half of the twentieth century. Then, we will identify some milestones that led to the demise of professional selling in the financial services sector.

Next, we will look at some of the reasons why many in our profession may be headed for hard times. In short, some of us are becoming progressively more irrelevant to our potential customers.

That decline is largely, although not entirely, due to technology. The popular term is "disruptive technology." We prefer our own term, *intrusion technology.*

Finally, being salesmen, we will give the reader a road map that will *provide a reason to celebrate a rosy future for financial service professionals.* Ironically, that path will be powered by technology.

We will also examine the emerging new environment and give readers a blend between the past and the future that will contain all the ingredients needed to succeed and prosper going forward. We even have a cookbook (sales process) that provides a proper blending of the lessons from our past with the contemporary dynamics needed for building today's successful financial services practice.

> *Before we travel the exciting road from potential irrelevance to indispensability, it is essential to understand how we achieved, and then lost, relevance in the first place.*

For many of today's producers, embracing this text may be the most difficult journey of their careers. For some, it's going to be just plain impossible. For the rest, we hope the logic and timing of our sales process, software, and philosophy will more than justify any of the necessary short-term pain.

We believe one of the keys to a rich future is being aware of and learning from our history. Thus, our first two chapters will discuss some past lessons at risk of being lost to the false notion that the rules of the game have changed. We submit that most have not.

We're going to prove to readers that, even though the game has indeed changed, the rules that matter are as important as ever!

After that comes the tough part: moving into the uncharted waters of the future—a future with a new playbook but the same basic rules, which at times may seem downright awkward.

With that admonition in mind, we're rooting for every person who takes the pledge to avoid irrelevance and commit to becoming indispensable.

When Selling Became a Profession

In our view, the golden age of selling occurred in the United States from the post–World War II period until the turn of the millennium. As most of us know, it was a period of unprecedented economic growth and prosperity.

The most significant economic result of this period was that, for the first time, the typical American family had something called "discretionary income"—money available to be spent or saved as they wished. *People spent this money mostly on what seemed like luxuries at the start but what eventually became necessities.*

The world of marketing, especially advertising, exploded (think *Mad Men*). With it, a new era in the realm of sales began. There were more opportunities to be a salesman than to be just about any other type of professional. Dad on the hit TV show *Father Knows Best* was an insurance salesman. *Death of a Salesman* was a runaway hit on Broadway.

During this period, dozens of sales training companies emerged, all offering secrets to unlock one's sales potential. There were also hundreds of books written on sales, marketing, and the like. Most were written for baby boomers, just out of college and looking for a career with the kind of unlimited income and little or no capital investment that commissioned selling offered.

The gold standard of sales training courses was the Dale Carnegie Sales Course. And the gold standard of sales training books was the textbook they used to teach that course. Published in 1959, *The Five Great Rules of Selling*, by Percy H. Whiting, was a huge hit. In this book, Mr. Whiting brilliantly breaks down the complicated process of selling any product into five steps. The book then goes on to provide a detailed analysis of each step. Even today, one must admit that he pretty much nailed it.

> ➤ **Attention.** Salespeople need first to get prospects' attention, or else there is no next step.
> ➤ **Interest.** Getting the prospect's interest is a recurring step in the sales process—interested enough to give us

an appointment, interested enough to listen to our questions and answer them, and interested enough to consider a next step.

➤ **Desire.** There are several other **emotion-based** words and phrases that are subordinate to this one, all of which can be reasons for buying: need, greed, status, peace of mind, and fear of loss, to mention a few.

➤ **Conviction.** We all know that emotion sells, but that's not what makes for a satisfied client. In Mr. Whiting's classic primer, *conviction* means justifying your purchase with facts and logic.

➤ **Close.** This is the step that ruled through the 1970s, the old challenge of answering objections. It was a cottage industry in the world of selling when we were beginning our careers. As we'll discuss later, it's an outdated term. *Today, if you need to close, you've already lost the sale.*

The reason this book was so popular, and why it still has value today, is that it gives us our first lesson in attaining relevance:

Remember—we couldn't become irrelevant[1] without first becoming relevant!

The Financial Industry National Regulatory Authority (FINRA) has a very important rule. They call it the "know your customer" rule. They're spot-on with that. Almost every continuing education class we are required to take reminds us of this helpful rule that, if followed, will not only keep us out of trouble but also help us become more successful in our profession.

Back in the days of Dale Carnegie's sales classes, we were

---

[1] *Note:* Most of our readers are not "irrelevant" or anything close to it. We use the term in this guide to draw attention to the overwhelming evidence that there are forces moving us in the direction of irrelevancy—forces that, if ignored, could indeed have their way with us!

taught a very similar rule, long before it became a regulatory guidepost. We think FINRA's rule would be stickier if they used it the way we learned it at our Dale Carnegie Sales Course:

"You can sell John Jones what John Jones buys if you can see John Jones through John Jones's eyes."

This training course was the first time anyone tried to break down the steps for making a sale, much like touching the bases in baseball. If you miss one of them, you don't score. So, you could go back after a missed sale and think about where you lost it and how you could do better next time. "At which step did I lose the prospect?"

As we all know, the weaker the salesperson, the harder the process is on him or her. The Dale Carnegie Sales Course was the first to point out that if you don't make the sale, it is probably *not because you aren't a good closer*. It is more likely that you didn't arouse *desire* or evoke *conviction*. Today we call that discovery.

Another thing that is both correct and groundbreaking about Mr. Whiting's book is that it recognizes that making a sale is really a *series of sales*. The better you are at each step, the easier the next step will be—until the close would become, as one early pundit put it, "mechanical."

It was a process. That was a big deal in the 1970s world of selling! After all, this was at a time when other best-selling books were all about closing the sale. One memorable best seller was titled *The Sale Begins When the Customer Says No*, by Elmer G Letterman. That was true old school.

Yet it too was relevant because, for most salespeople in those days, *successful closing was defined by prevailing in a contest of wills. Today such an approach would be a formula for failure.*

All the same, there were limitations to the rules set out in *The Five Great Rules of Selling*. Most notably, it was a *linear process*. This meant the prospects had to pretty much know their lines! Or to use the language of the day, it was very close to a "canned sales talk." And that's why we start our journey to relevance by looking at it.

You see, the first thing we want to learn from the past of selling is to *become destined to repeat some of it, as opposed to being condemned to repeating all of it.*

Yes, millennial readers, you can learn from those who've walked before you! And your first lesson is that most sales presentations are canned. Here's the catch: only those successful at it admit to it!

Most of the greats we know have a canned sales talk. We can tone it down if you prefer and say that they have a selling process, a process that they follow, just like a baseball player, not only by touching all the bases to score but also by taking every step before that: preparing to get into the batter's box, assuming the right stance. Like any good sales talk, all but the more alert fans are unaware of the discipline and preparation that goes into the process. So, it is with professional selling. The analogy is sound.

By the way, you are going to encounter a lot of analogies, metaphors, and similes on our journey to indispensability. So, let's clear up what we mean by a *canned sales talk* with another analogy.

Many of us read Shakespeare in college. For some of us, it may as well have been written in Mandarin. That's probably true of a lot of plays. Plays are written to be performed, not read during halftime breaks, which is what many of us students did. There's a reason it's called theater—a live performance brings the story and characters to life.

If you've seen a few Shakespearean plays, you know that most great performers become known for "their Othello" or "their Hamlet"—same lines, but different interpretations leading to different performances, sometimes dramatically different. It's all in the interpretation of the character and, of course, knowing your material so well that it's anything but canned.

If that's too cerebral, think of Johnny Depp's Captain Jack Sparrow in the hugely successful Disney film franchise *Pirates of the Caribbean*. He didn't change a word in the script, but he created an interpretation of the character that not only floored but also terrified the directors and writers. They remained in dismay until the box office results started rolling in. That role earned Mr. Deep a spot in the actors' pantheon of great character interpreters and developers.

Great salespeople are the same. They don't just learn their lines. They learn from experience how to bring those words to life for their prospects. They give life and meaning to simple words and phrases. They create word pictures (interest) that evoke emotion (desire). Then, they show factually grounded numbers that provide logic (conviction).

In short:

We sell by using words, pictures, and numbers.

In that order. More on this later.

Doing the right things right, however, takes more hours of preparation than the typical salesperson usually puts into even the most important presentations. Therein lies one of the key differences between irrelevance and indispensability. That said, it is critical the reader understand that there is one very big difference between acting and selling.

We are not, nor should we become, actors. Yet many salespeople are actors, and that's why they fail. That may sound contradictory, but here's the fundamental issue: not Shakespeare, not the internet, and not the authors of this guide to indispensability are responsible for the creation of your sales process.

Only you can be the author of your character.

And *character* is the operative word here. *Your character can be an ideal version of yourself, but it still must be based upon who you really are. Not on who you wish you were, or who you think the prospect would like you to be, but on who you are, right down to your core values.*

How do we know this?

We all know that the greats in the world of selling know their product, believe in their product, and seek out prospects who will genuinely benefit from their product.[2] They also believe that their services will benefit the client, well beyond the economic rewards that go to the salesperson.

We bring these well-known facts up for a painful reason. You've probably heard this quote, but it's worth reinforcing for our purposes here:

> The primary difference between successful people and failures is that successful people do those things that failures aren't willing to.

Our favorite version of the same message is this:

> Successful people do all those things others won't, until they are able do all those things that others can't.

Here's the painful part: our requirements at FSN are stiff, so we don't have the batting average we'd like.

Unfortunately, many people in our profession either lack the resolve or simply don't have the ability to do what we ask of them. That is probably an unusual statement for a book about successful selling, but these are unusual times.

---

[2] When we say *product*, we are speaking generically. As we shall see, today, more than ever, *it is your expertise and specialization that is your actual product.*

For those who do have the resolve and the ability, there's only one thing needed to open the door to your future: *know-how.*

The authors of this book are well into our eighth decade of life, and most of it has been spent learning or teaching the things we share in these pages. Much of it we learned the hard way. We have a collective abundance of know-how that well exceeds the time we have to pass it around.

We might add that *much of that know-how comes from scar tissue rather than muscle—a learning formula we'd like to spare our students from.* It is our hope that the FSN Client Acquisition Process is the most efficient way to avoid unnecessary mistakes.

For now, this guide is a first step. If you not only read it but also study it, you'll be a lot closer than you may think to vocational fulfillment as an adviser.

The Situation is the Boss!

One of our mentors, the great management trainer Garry Kinder, used to tell us, "In today's world, you are not the boss. I am not the boss. Nor is anyone else. *The situation is the boss!*" For those of us selling financial products and services, we have a situation on our hands!

How do we know?

It's becoming clear that some of the things we know about performance-based compensation in the world of selling are changing. We aren't telling you anything you aren't already hearing about, even if you haven't quite processed its meaning for your future.

We can blame the Department of Labor, the hundreds of online competitors, Turbo Advisor, the decline of family values, or whatever impetus of change we choose. As we shall discuss later, we don't know for sure what changes to our compensation are on the horizon. All the same, going forward we are suggesting FSPs get ahead of the curve and sell as if there were total transparency in everything they do.

There is current discussion that the built-in feature of several of our products known as a load or commission may be replaced by a fee schedule, similar to what doctors have experienced with nationalized health care. There's even talk that our compensation on some products may be part of the contracts clients purchase, like the warning label on certain commercial products.

These changes may come from several sources: some from the product providers themselves, some from SROs (self-regulating organizations), and some from the various governmental and oversight agencies.

What this means to you is that the adviser is becoming a value-added option. Prospects may only pay us for the value we add to their purchase and if they feel it's in their best interests to engage us.

For some that thought is terrifying. Others may say, "Bring it on. I'm worth what I earn, and I don't mind going public with it!"

We feel these current and future realities could impede some FSPs in their efforts to grow their practices. If people know exactly what they are paying for our services, they will need to feel we are worth it.

Here's a hint:

> *If you feel you are worth what the client pays for your services, you are halfway to not being materially affected by future changes in compensation.*

For the FSP who feels comfortable with what we ask of him or her in this guide, we submit that these potentially dramatic changes we've been hearing about may not be as challenging as they appear. It's mostly a matter of perspective.

As those who know us are aware, *we think perspective is one of the biggest words in the English language.*

In short, you're still going to be paid in direct proportion to your effort and ability. It's just that it won't be decided by you alone. It may be more the result of what your industry and customers feel you're worth.

Ideally, they'll feel you're a bargain. How to elicit the conclusion from your clients that you are indispensable is something we will address throughout this guide.

We suggested earlier that we all need a sales process, but it cannot seem even remotely canned. We mentioned that character is going to come into play. That's because we think most FSPs are about to come face-to-face with their own stated principles.

Here's our question:

Do you believe that you offer prospects something that is worth not only the price they pay but also the additional premium they pay for having you attached to it?

From our *perspective*, you won't make the cut unless you are selling a service that you honestly believe is a good deal for your prospect. For it to work, however, your prospect must not only feel it is a good deal for her but also be happy about you being part of it.

Both conditions must be present for you to be a credible, and therefore an indispensable, component of the client's buying process.

Let's start by examining the metrics of the type of selling that a few of us who are still around were trained on.

The biggest problem with traditional selling is not the process but the flow of it. As we have pointed out, it's linear—five consecutive steps.

Today, few prospects know their lines. Even fewer want to be "sold" anything. Yet we keep emphasizing that salespeople need a process. Let's think outside the old selling box and look at things from the prospect's point of view.

For our prospects, the FSN Client Acquisition Process is not linear at all. It's dynamic. It may be both vertical and horizontal. By that we mean that it may be the FSP facilitating or controlling the process at one moment, whereas it may be the prospect calling the shots at another. We must learn to engage the prospect's participation in the process. If we don't, we risk the following:

Against our advice, prospects may "try this at home" using online services.

This would not be a concern to begin with were it not for the fact that most of our readers are too young to have been trained on the five-step linear process we've been discussing. This process, flawed though it may have been, introduced a concept that was brand new in the 1970s.

That concept was then known as *needs-based selling*.

As we'll see later, we must get back to a contemporary version of these roots before we make progress toward indispensability.

The idea we propose is that people must have and recognize a problem before deciding to proceed with our recommendations.

If you think that's old news, you don't know what's going on around you as well as you may think.

Here's our question:

> *Do you believe that most of the life insurance, investment, and annuity products being sold today are being purchased with a problem as the dominant buying motive?*

We don't want to go so far as to say that greed has replaced need, but we have a strong belief, especially with sales involving insurance:

> *An insurable need or significant objective must be agreed to before product performance is discussed. The failure to make certain that the prospects understand their needs has become a much bigger issue than most of us realize.*

Those who sell financial products are in an arena that leaves most other salespeople behind. Ours is the world of the most difficult kind of selling, and those who succeed are arguably the best of the best. If an adviser can sell something you cannot see, feel, or touch, he or she will be successful selling just about anything.

Here's our question:

What do we really sell?

Isn't it just promises on a piece of paper? In many cases, it's not even that. It's just educated guesses that depend upon multiple variables that no one can control, let alone predict with accuracy.

Since we are more insurance guys than anything else, we're going to focus on FSPs who offer not only investments but also life insurance, long-term care, and related mortality and morbidity products such as annuities.

Carrying our earlier baseball analogy a little further, no hitter ever diminished his power by practicing his swing with a leaded bat before stepping up to the plate.

No offense to those selling other products, *but life insurance guys always have to use a leaded bat!*

If life insurance is not a primary part of your practice, you will still want to stay tuned. We promise you won't be bored.

We believe any FSP who implements our strategies may well achieve indispensability, whether they ever swing the leaded life insurance bat or not!!

From Commonplace to Relevant

The Five Great Rules of Selling spawned a new era in world of sales. As we have mentioned, instead of selling a product for just its features and benefits, the world of doing fact-finding and discovering needs was born. At the same time, the earliest financial planners sold mutual funds, life insurance, annuities, and similar products as part of a plan for family security. These were also needs based. The important development was this:

Not only were we now selling an intangible, but also the customers were not buying it for the here and now. They were buying it for some time in the future.

Needs-based selling meant planning for events down the road. Instead of a stock or a bond trade that you could avoid telling your spouse about, or maybe even make a killing on, it was a mutual fund for a rainy day. Instead of burial insurance in case you dropped dead, people bought a lot of insurance that was part of a bigger plan for the long-term security of their families.

Needs-based selling also addressed things like the kids' college education, paying off the mortgage early, emergencies caused by illness or disability, saving for a vacation, or even for something as far out as retirement. These were all things most people couldn't afford to think about before the economic explosion that accompanied the baby boomer generation.

Suddenly, there were growing families and growing incomes. With that came growing obligations and attainable long-term financial goals.

With the need for families to plan, not only for the

unexpected, with insurance, but also for the expected, with savings and investments, the financial services industry enjoyed explosive growth.

On the selling side, needs-based sales training replaced product pushing. Selling systems were developed by major insurance companies and stock brokerage firms. Other industries also provided extensive sales training.

For example, Xerox Corp (now a casualty because of its failure to adapt) developed a selling system called PSS (Professional Sales System), which was so successful that they sold it to other sales forces, including several insurance and stock brokerage firms. It was built around strategic questioning and skillful listening.

> *Selling life insurance and individual mutual funds had, at last, become a profession—a profession that was* relevant *to society and to the economy!*

Over time, however, the greatest success in developing sales training systems came from some of the leading producers in the sales forces.

Some readers are old enough to remember Financial Needs Analysis, the one-card system, and funnel talk, just to mention three. All were developed by legendary salesmen. The objectives were primarily to uncover needs, create customer awareness of problems, and then, lo and behold, show the customer a product that solved the problem. Even though that product was somewhat of a hammer in search of a nail, it was still far better than anything offered prior.

For most of us, a lot has changed since then. For others, not so much. The most striking example is with a handful of old-line mutual life companies that convince their sales force a single product is the cure-all for most any accumulation or protection need, a tactic we believe is an anachronism waiting to be exposed. More on this later.

In keeping with our commitment to full disclosure, we now must pause to make a point we'd rather not dwell upon.

In the early days of selling life insurance and doing financial plans over the kitchen table, the product delivery system was burdensome, to say the least. The high turnover among early producers selling intangibles was huge. Yet since we knew that these products weren't bought but had to be sold, the industry endured their very costly product delivery systems.

The expenses for the delivery systems of insurance and mutual funds had to be borne by the product. That didn't help with anyone taking an objective look at product performance. As a result, the argument for alternative ways of achieving a similar result, like "buy term and invest the difference," became epidemic.

> *Life insurance was a classic case of a product that is effective but not efficient.*

The salespeople of the day who became successful were those who *adapted*. This is a word that will be crucial throughout our quest for indispensability.

Advisers adapted by focusing on the features and benefits of the product, rather than the numbers. This is a partial reason why needs-based selling was developed.

Today, we have a much more noble reason to return to this approach and to use it going forward. Ironically, it's not to divert attention from the less than glamorous financial performance of the products, but rather to understand our prospects—perhaps for the first time.

For those who weren't around during the period we've been reviewing, you may have a daunting task ahead.

How do we know?

First, because needs-based selling took the difficulty of selling intangibles to a new level. Not only did you have to sell promises and guesses on a piece of paper, but also the intent was for a result that may not have be realized for years, if not decades. Who can sell stuff like that? Well, it wasn't a field for amateurs or the tenderhearted.

It has been called the golden era for those selling financial products for a reason. We were paid well—some of us extraordinarily well. The products we sold were also complex and difficult, if not seemingly impossible, for consumers to fully understand.

Full disclosure: a lot of the salespeople didn't understand them either!

Most middle-class and affluent Americans knew they should own life insurance. What young family head doesn't think he should have life insurance to protect his earning power and plan for his kids' education or his eventual retirement?

As one great sales trainer of the day used to say, "Most people know what they need to do and ought to do, but they usually choose to do what they want to do and feel like doing!"

Persuading people to do the right thing has always been easier said than done.

Implementing a plan that called for the purchase of insurance, mutual funds, and savings vehicles was an act of responsibility. It took prudence and foresight to sacrifice the immediate gratification from hard-earned dollars in exchange for future and perhaps uncertain benefits.

These were character purchases, and it took advisers who cultivated similar values to win the confidence of the saver, investor, and insurance buyer.

The considerable difficulties of finding the right kind of prospect and then convincing her of her needs became what we like to call *the things that make us necessary.*

The financial institutions that manufactured the products knew this. Back then, we may not have been indispensable, but those who sold financial products had achieved relevance. And so it was throughout the sixties and seventies.

Why are we taking the time to review this ancient history? First, it is our belief that *it may be easier to return to one's roots than to plant a seed while on the run. And those who are stuck on selling proposals, instead of discovering problems, will, in our opinion, soon be on the run!*

Second, we want to give the reader the backdrop to 1980, when something happened that changed everything.

Actually, it was two things that happened. Almost simultaneously.

Both had a lasting impact, which was to put the sales forces of the life insurance industry in a protracted state of decline over the next three decades.

Because that brings us all the way to today, we believe visiting these events will help us prepare for what lies ahead.

Rao-ism #64

I don't know what the future holds, but I know who holds the future!

How We Surrendered Our Hard-Earned Relevance

The most closely guarded secret of the financial services industry is hidden in plain sight; time has an impact on the value of money that greatly exceeds the role most of us assign to the end result.

—Gary Schulte, *The Fall of First Executive*

IT'S HARD to call any trend that has lasted thirty years and counting a trend at all, let alone a disastrous one, since disasters occur overnight rather than over decades, and especially since many of those who ultimately will suffer the consequences of that trend have experienced careers of unprecedented prosperity.

Yet that's exactly what has happened for many financial product salespeople over the past thirty years. For the industry, it has been a slow-motion train wreck!

Having said that, we believe that for many FSPs, our industry is on the cusp of one of the most promising eras we have witnessed in our careers.

If that sounds contradictory, it's because it only looks good for some of us.

The products of the financial services industry tend to be long term. They grow slowly but steadily. Be it the mortgage portfolio of a bank, an iconic family of mutual funds, or a block of policies in a life insurance company, each tends to disintermediate the same way.

At least that's how it always was, until the meltdown of 2008.

Those problems, although more than a decade behind us, are a part of why we are entering a new era of compensation for those selling financial products. The good news is that within that transformation lies *an elegant solution for anyone with the resolve, ability, and know-how to adapt to the situation.*

We'll unwrap that gift in the coming chapters.

First, we must conclude our history lesson so that we are fully equipped to move forward with our eyes wide open.

Back to the two developments that changed everything in the Evolutionary Eighties. Most readers already know what they are, but that's not the point of our discussion. It's the impact they had on our profession that matters here.

First was the unbundling of financial products so that the investment features became easier to sell under favorable economic conditions—and a lot easier to sell than the need for a death benefit!

Second was what we will just call sales technology, which is a catchall term for something that has had a sweeping effect on all of us over the past thirty years.

The former is primarily universal life and similar current assumption products. The latter includes everything from printed illustrations to the internet and, now, algorithms that extrapolate performance and events into the future.

Of course, we can't forget online advice, which is ostensibly dedicated to our obsolescence.

What is important to our discussion is the following:

These two developments were devastating to the progress that financial product salespeople had made in the previous decades.

That's why the history lesson in Chapter 1 is important to our story.

We had learned to do needs-based selling. No, it wasn't financial planning or tax planning or estate planning, but it was still dramatic progress.

We had achieved relevance in the financial services industry. In the process, we learned to do something that was groundbreaking at the time: *We learned to sell by asking questions and uncovering real problems.*

We learned to identify a single need, which we naively called a "hot button." We used things like economic statistics, pie charts, asset allocation, dollar cost averaging, human life values, and morbidity and mortality statistics to provide the justification (conviction) for our proposals.

These were not merely financial plans. They were reasonable plans that solved *one problem at a time.* Keep that in mind, as it will be central to your coming indispensability.

The two juggernauts mentioned above eventually ended all that for most of us. The focus had shifted from the long-term benefits of the character purchase we described earlier to a shorter-term sale that was driven by economic performance of the product.

Our harshest critics have claimed we went from selling need to selling greed.

What we forgot to consider along the way was this:

In a product-driven environment, the role of the salesperson can be greatly diminished.

How do we know?

The very first universal life products paid little or no

commissions. The actuaries thought these products performed so well that they'd grow legs and walk into the prospects' arms (figuratively).

As it turned out, they did need sales reps, not only to sell the product but also to find the premium dollars to buy it by replacing traditional whole life.

Eventually, full commissions were paid by most companies, even on their internal replacements.

That was a moment that did not portend well for things to come.

With all of that, many of us lost our unique ability. *We surrendered some of the things that made us necessary.* Nowhere was this more evident than at the point of sale with a universal life policy. Most of you don't need a tutorial on the subject, so we will just point out the most disastrous consequences to the financial adviser.

In a nutshell:

> *When short-term interest rates spiked out of control (i.e., when the prime rate hit 20 percent), we extrapolated them over the lifetime of the financial world's longest-term product—life insurance.*

The thing about this colossal blunder that interests us is the impact it had on the adviser.

That may sound heartless, but as much as the consumer and the carriers lost, the salespeople paid the ultimate price. They had taken the first step toward losing their hard-earned relevance.

This came not only from selling unrealistic short-term returns in a long-term product but also from a much bigger windfall that, at first blush, was a salesperson's dream come true.

Agents didn't even have to ask for a check to close the sale! All they had to do was explain that this new miracle product was so amazing that, for the same premium dollar the customers had been paying, they could have twice as much insurance. Or, if they preferred, they could keep the same amount of insurance and pay half their current premium. Of course, the better salespeople would then sell some other product to absorb the "savings" from the replacement.

These daring new products, which were a direct result of strange economic times, brought tremendous collateral damage with them. Most of the new products created a stark mismatch between assets and liabilities for several major institutions. That devastation hurt not only those doing the selling but also the consumer (as told in one of our other books).

As irresponsible as these sales practices may have seemed, they might never have gained so much traction without the second juggernaut provided by early sales technology.

The perfectly timed sales innovation delivered by technology was the ledger statement or product illustration. It was a godsend for sales reps.

The ledger statement appeared for the first time, showing printed columns that projected product performance. Until then, advisers had relied upon their administrative staffs to type up summary sheets showing product performance at various durations. We'd show global performance at ages, like age thirty-five, forty-five, and fifty-five.

Because most salespeople in those days couldn't afford clerical support, many (including us) usually wrote our proposals in longhand on a legal pad. These sales presentations were known as the "tic-tac-toe"— "Here's what you put in. Here's what you get out. Here's when and how you get it: live, die, or quit."

Now the companies or their minions would provide advisers with unprecedented credibility by printing illustrations under *their name and logo*, showing product performance year by year.

Perhaps the most amazing thing of all was that the adviser could plug in his own assumed interest rate—the agent's assumed rate, not that of the company!

All this came with the unprecedented credibility that a company-sanctioned ledger brought to the point of sale.

Eventually the companies put caps on the rates that were illustrated, but they were generous caps, so generous that the projected performance on some classes of policy would allow the planned premium to *permanently vanish after as little as six years.*

These developments were a mind-numbing breakthrough.

> *We could sell the only product in all of the financial world that was as good as we were willing to say it was!*

One can't help but wonder how credible those illustrations would have looked to consumers if they were scratched onto the legal pads many of us had previously used!

Thus, needs-based selling gave way to two simple questions: "Do you own any life insurance? Really! Tell me, is it the old kind or the new kind?" And the new kind was essentially free.

Eventually, most of those vanishing premiums "unvarnished." Along with them, some of the less prudent insurance companies also vanished. In fact, by the end of the eighties, these practices led to such a mismatch between assets and liabilities that several major life insurance companies got into serious trouble for the first time in their history.

Four of the ten largest life insurance companies had to be stabilized by regulators and either put into receivership or merged into other large companies.

The response to the crisis by the insurance companies was to get these massive liabilities of their own making off their balance sheets.

How?

Transfer the risk to the customer!

Thus, began the explosion of variable life, whereby the asset in the life insurance policy was no longer managed by the insurance company but, rather, by money managers at mutual funds and similar institutions.

It is important to pause and note that although the customer's interests were not necessarily the primary motive for the promotion of this product, it has generally been good for consumers in the long run. Variable life continues today to be an excellent choice for those who have an insurable need and are in the right situation.

But, that's not the whole story.

To get the clients out of what now became the "new 'old kind' of policy," namely, universal life and other forms of interest-sensitive products, companies had to again turn to the sales force to roll their books of business a second time. That became the windfall for agents of the 1990s.

Or so it seemed.

By now, many advisers were getting farther and farther away from needs-based selling and the prospecting skills that accompany it. For them, after the rollovers were complete, things just became more difficult.

Many moved in the direction of selling annuities and other accumulation products, while an even larger number moved into financial planning.

Saved by the consumer again! To the good fortune of many life agents, both annuities and financial planning were really exploding onto the scene, and consumers were in need of qualified advisers.

Why is all this important to your future? To remind you that, through these challenges, *insurance-based advisers and financial planners showed a remarkable ability for adapting to change.*

For those who were there, we believe that trait is why many of you are going to be just fine in the coming years.

There's just one more problem we must face before turning our attention to the rosy future that we promise is in store for some of our readers.

Everything we've discussed so far takes us to a point where advisers have bounced around, or been bounced around, in an industry that has, in many ways, struggled to find its identity. In the process, for all we've gained and then lost, most have demonstrated that they are survivors. How that has happened is something for which we don't have a complete explanation, but we're pretty sure a big part of it is their skill as salespeople.

As we pointed out earlier, people who sell financial products are the best salespeople in the world. Despite all the disruption of the past years, they still are the best. That's a good thing, because the coming transition we face could be our greatest challenge yet. Of course, for many of us, challenge has always spelled opportunity.

While we were letting our needs-based selling skills slip away, technology was picking up the slack. The internet. Online brokerage. Direct marketing.

At the turn of the millennium, we began to hear about the supposedly self-directed consumer. The list of tools at their disposal has grown every year since.

Fast-forward to today, and there is even solid evidence that artificial intelligence is here. Among its earliest targets will likely be financial advice. The logical demographic for artificial intelligence will be the client of the middle-market financial adviser.

The technology that once leveraged their credibility with

instant computer-generated illustrations and client access to all their investments plans now becomes the tail that wags the dog.

Not good.

The institutions clearly want to believe that there is nothing the adviser can do that technology cannot do better. The manufacturers of our products are shedding no tears because they think they will finally control the customer they always felt they were entitled to own. We know you've read about this issue and talked with your peers about it for years. Our purpose here is to help you better understand how it all happened, so we can engineer an appropriate response.

Everyone is invited to come along, but as we shall soon learn, it's a journey only for those with the *strength, the smarts, and the ability to adapt* to a rapidly changing environment!

For starters, if our readers are on the same page as we are, they agree with this premise:

> *Technology is on a mission to make most of us irrelevant.*

In fact, in the eyes of the financial institutions that fund technology, they have already won the battle. Some think that the salespeople are just an anachronism they allow to hang around to shepherd in their electronic replacements.

More and more, clients are encouraged to use their own technology to establish bilateral connections with the institutions. To many, it's only a matter of time.

Maybe that's true, but FSN has a strategy that will allow many to not only survive but also flourish.

As fellow salespeople, our readers know we are not going to identify a problem unless we think we have a solution.

We believe that those who create the future must first understand the lessons of the past. That's why we needed our discussion in the first two chapters to set up the rollout of the FSN Sales Process.

FSN has a plan, and alert advisers are its centerpiece!

We have a plan that, as we have said from the start, probably won't work for all of our readers. Yet for some, it will change their lives for the better.

That is what we all want for our clients, and it's all we can hope to give to our students.

Rao-ism #57

You don't buy life insurance because you are going to die but because those whom you love are going to live.

THREE ESSENTIALS OF SUCCESS THAT NEVER CHANGE

It is not the strongest species who survive. Nor is it the smartest. It is those most adaptable to change.

—Charles Darwin, *On the Origin of the Species*

DARWIN WAS right about a lot of things. Unfortunately for us, the profession of selling has evolved to the point where the precept described above no longer applies. Yes, we too are convinced that to survive we must be able to adapt—and adapt big-time! But for all its virtue, adapting just to survive is not enough for the FSP of the future.

Why? First, because survival is not our goal.

It may be a benchmark in the challenging environment we are now entering, but it is hardly a destination.

Second, because adapting is a defensive strategy.

Again, we must be able to defend against not only the onslaught of technology, but also a host of other factors working to secure our irrelevance. Adaptation is crucial to our objective of indispensability, but it's not our endgame.

Darwin's lifelong work taught him that he could bet on one essential trait and win his place in history. We aren't so lucky.

We need to score in all three categories: strength, smarts, and adaptability.

Since the rest of this guide is intended for those who cultivate all three of these characteristics, let's look at each quality in the order Darwin presents them to us and see how they apply to us.

The Strongest

We must be strong to succeed in our business—strong in every sense of the word.

We must be strong enough to build our practice by carving out of thin air a population of clients who trust and respect us as their go-to source for financial advice.

We must be strong enough to build priceless relationships that cannot be replaced, not even by other humans, let alone electronic devices.

We must be strong enough to seek the counsel of mentors and be coachable, even taking advice that may seem counterintuitive.

We must be strong enough to break off chunks of Auto Advisor and beat him over the head with it!

> *Strength comes from confidence. Confidence comes from competence.*
>
> *Competence comes from study, experience, hard work, and having the right mentors.*

That's where the authors and our faculty at FSN come in. Our purpose for the rest of our time in this business is to share our wisdom and experience with those who follow us. We feel compelled to do so because of the dearth of mentors to the younger generation, as compared to when we were starting out.

Our goal is twofold:

> ➤ *First, to preserve those things that not only got us where we are but also have kept us there, so others can learn from our experience.*
> ➤ *Second, to help advisers let go of those things that are no longer part of the current realities we face, so they can adapt to a new way of selling financial services, specifically, the FSN Client Acquisition Process.*

From a vocational standpoint, these are times that will make or break many of us. These times will most certainly call for strength.

We must have strength to give up some of the fundamentals that have helped the established FSP get where he is today. For many of us, a major reason we came in to the business was to be compensated in direct proportion to our effort, our ability, and most importantly our results. This does not mean giving up on the ability to make the exceptional living that our industry has always offered. But things will change.

Some FSPs have a Pavlovian relationship with compensation. Making the sale is like ringing a bell and getting a commission check is the reward. For those, we think there are better opportunities elsewhere.

Most of us believe that our greatest motivation and vocational fulfillment comes from seeing the benefit of our work in action, contributing to the well-being of a client. For us, the upcoming changes should not have a lasting impact on compensation.

If we can put just one item between ourselves and the financial rewards of our work, we'll be fine, no matter what the changes in compensation may be. Those who know what that item is, even before hearing it, are those to whom we are talking.

The welfare of the client is the first and, by far, the most dominant value of today's successful FSP. Leading with that conviction every day takes strength!

The Things We Believe in Never Change!

IF YOU want to put all the pending changes in compensation and related issues into a single sentence, try this: Sell, live, and stand by *the golden rule*. This point is worth a brief story that brings comfort to those of us struggling with all the rapid changes going on in our industry and, for that matter, our world.

> Shortly after the end of World War II, there was serious talk about asking General Douglas MacArthur to run for president. The problem was that he'd been away from the United States for over a decade, dealing with issues in the Pacific and specifically the Philippines. He was perceived by some to be out of touch with the USA.
>
> So, the convention delegates paid him a visit. They told him he needed to return home and learn about the many important changes going on. They insisted that everything had changed and changed dramatically, saying that he must come home and learn about the new things happening, so he could share his current beliefs with the public, based upon all that had changed. His response was classic MacArthur:
>
> "Gentlemen, *the things I believe in never change.*"

When it came to strength, MacArthur had few rivals. Yet *he adapted* to a lot of change when he was in the Philippines for all those years. The things that really mattered to him were, no doubt, a big help.

What this means to you is that strength and adapting to change can be compatible so long as you keep your core values in order.

> *The golden rule: clients first. The rest will take care of itself.*
>
> *Those things that never change!*

It's seldom easy, but if you can visualize and if you can imagine, then you can adapt. The kind of strength we are calling for involves things like values, emotions, character, and resolve, rather than physical strength. If we have the desire to do so, most of us can muster up those qualities.

Smarts are another matter.

The Smartest

Along with being strong, you must be smart to appreciate and benefit from the FSN Sales Process.

Unlike intelligence, which is usually static, your smarts are a function of what you do with your life experience.

If you're not sure you are smart enough to be an FSN adviser, you may not be. Before you check out, however, you may want to hear more about our definition of *smart*.

In our view, you can be intelligent without being smart, but you can't be smart without being intelligent.

Unfortunately, some of the smartest people we know don't think of themselves as intelligent because they may lack the education that usually accompanies intelligence.

Education is important, but we all know people who are educated beyond their level of intelligence.

There's no substitute for street smarts.

Here's another of our beliefs that may seem a contradiction in terms:

Experience is a better teacher than education.

How do we know?

Because experience is personal, not third party, and therefore hard to ignore. Experience is also usually one-trial learning. Most of us got our smarts from experience (getting burned) rather than from education (being lectured). Some, like our students, are lucky enough to have the benefit of both.

If you plan to become a member of our network, education will be important, but being smart is a requirement.

The things we teach come from our experience and must be not only learned but also mastered. After all, the situation is the boss, and the situation is that we don't have a lot of time to get ahead of the curve on technology and regulation.

The impact of combining experience with education is the reason we have a series of intense courses that accompany this guide. If you enroll, we hope to become not only your teachers but also, for some, your mentors.

Since we don't give homework assignments or administer tests, the tool that pulls everything in this guide and our network together is within you. It's your mind.

It's how you process information, develop procedures, and implement a plan of action. We're not talking about putting together an action plan in a ring binder. Support for those kinds of mechanics and exercises abounds from the journeymen wholesalers who offer seminars and summits throughout our industry. Some even claim to be our competition. To be sure, the things we teach have some imitators, but remember smarts come from experience. Experience is our syllabus.

As you will soon see, we provide tools you won't find anywhere else. We teach techniques with proprietary language that we have crafted over the decades. One of the things you'll experience at our events is something we are especially proud of. Our programs include an all-star faculty, with the experience and résumés seldom found on one forum. We also have a strict requirement for all our faculty: *no holdbacks!*

How often have you heard a wonderful presentation from a great FSP telling story after story of what he or she did? We enjoy those presentations as much as the next person, but if the person doesn't tell you *how* he or she did it, it's only entertainment.

We're not talking about an eloquent flow of the transaction complete with Excel spreadsheets either. That's just more entertainment.

We get down and dirty with our case examples. In fact, we usually have an FSN member as part of our presentation. You don't need to hear about what we did. You need to know how a student whom we shared a case with did it—not only what she observed and learned from what we did, but also how we did it, step by step, in bite-size, digestible pieces.

> *At our training events, we make the magic sauce from scratch, mistakes and all.*

Again, we never allow ourselves, or any of our faculty, to have any holdbacks. Everything we have to give our students is theirs the minute they join FSN.

This is a two-way street.

Our organization is one of the premier networks because members can't have holdbacks either! Members are expected to share their best practices with their fellow FSPs. If you are not willing to do this, membership in FSN is not for you.

The creativity and resolve needed to make what you will learn your own is up to you. That takes some smarts.

Our hope is that our students will interpret our material and design a personalized version of it that has their thumb-prints and personalities all over it. As you'll hear us say many times, we compose the music, and our students write their own lyrics.

Of course, you will want to balance that statement with the oversight and review of your compliance officer or other appropriate supervisors.

Our teachings focus on the human elements—communication skills and strong personal relationships—not on products, product performance, or product providers. Those things are just fuel for the strategies we create and are not to be confused with the reason the client moves forward with a proposal.

Your mission to achieve indispensability is just that. It's yours, not ours. We are just your guides on the journey. Each FSP has a different destination.

The result is a creative combination of our experience and your objectives.

Remember that statement, because it is also a pillar of the selling process we are going to acquaint you with in the following pages.

All of that is going to take smarts.

The Most Adaptable

We agree with Darwin that when it comes to anything that is evolving, whether it evolves as slowly as a mammal or as fast as a microchip, the one trait needed to ensure survival is the ability to adapt. Otherwise:

We run the risk of using all our strength and all our smarts to become the very best at all those things that no longer work!

That's not likely to produce a favorable outcome in the jungle of life.

We have already covered the fact that, eventually, you're going to have to adapt to a different way of being paid for your work. Let's be clear, however: there are two situations going on with the business of charging fees, one being mandatory and the other being voluntary.

The former are the general trends originating in the regulatory and government agency arena. There is a worldwide movement to do away with commissions and move toward fees, wrap accounts, and the like. We know changes are coming for many products we currently sell, but we are not ready to concede that commissions for life insurance will be done away with anytime soon.

When and if we feel that mandatory fees are on the short-term horizon for various products, we'll be there with coaching advice learned from our many friends in other countries who have lived (and survived) in a fee-based environment.

For our purposes, when we mention fees, we do so because of our adamant belief that advisers using our sales process should charge a significant fee for their advice—voluntarily.

Then, as the landscape on commissions changes, our students will be well ahead of the competition. In the meantime, the type of proposed solutions we can produce with our interactive client tools more than justifies a reasonable fee. We think you'll agree.

Ironically, the next most important thing you must adapt to is learning to refuse to adapt blindly. Remember our discussion about how the blessing of technology gave us instant credibility with product illustrations that depicted financial performance that would otherwise be hard to believe?

Computer-generated output has been the opioid that drew us away from needs-based and client-based relationships, into a world of spreadsheets and projections.

In the process we learned something interesting: if you make the numbers look good enough, they can often evoke almost as strong the emotional response that those words and diagrams describing deeply held values once did.

It is a lot less work too! After all, conjuring up avarice as a buying motive is far simpler than finding needs, uncovering problems, and highlighting the long-term consequences of imprudent and selfish behavior. So most of us happily adapted to the Pied Piper of intrusion technology. In the process, we began our journey toward likely irrelevance.

Now, many of us feel the need to back away from those sales practices.

How you can do that is the subject of the balance of this guide.

One thing we don't want to do is to throw the proverbial baby out with the bathwater.

We are all familiar with the many ways technology has been an asset. It has eliminated many tedious functions that used to be done manually. In fact, without it, we never would have achieved much of our current value with clients.

No one can realistically dispute that. Our issue with technology is that we must draw the line between ally and interloper.

Here's our question:

How do we position ourselves in an era when technology is on the precipice of creating the financial advisory equivalent of the driverless car?

We may not have the complete answer, but we do know how to be sure you hold on to the wheel!

At FSN it is our goal to engage the best resources in the world of technology with a single purpose in mind: the creation of a platform that provides every tool imaginable to support our only customer, the FSP.

This commitment is irreversible and ongoing. Unlike the product providers and financial institutions that feign support for the FSP while they hedge their bets with Auto Advisor, we're all in.

When it comes to the long term, we cannot predict what the delivery system for financial advice is going to look like. That's because one thing we've learned by looking for long-term solutions is that no one seems to have a prevailing vision.

In fact, having done a lot of consulting in our careers, we notice that the long-term planning consultants are nowhere to be found. The only planning we are seeing has to do with adapting to change.

No magic bullets.

What we do know for sure is that we have a contemporary strategy for achieving indispensability as a provider of financial service products and advice. For those who choose to adapt the FSN Client Acquisition Process, *we will strive for success, prosperity, and vocational fulfillment.*

That said, keep in mind that nothing is forever, not even indispensability. Then again, if you follow our path to becoming a contemporary FSP, you may not need forever.

Rao-ism #46

Education is not about information; it's about transformation.

PART 2

THE THREE GREAT SKILLS OF THE MASTERS

In part 1 we covered *The Five Great Rules of Selling*—namely, the five steps that must be completed for a *successful sale to occur.*

Now we are going to discuss the three most important things that an FSP must excel at for a *successful career to occur.*

We call these the Three Great Skills of the Masters:

> ➢ prospecting and marketing (P&M)
> ➢ opening cases
> ➢ discovery

PROSPECTING AND MARKETING

Your prospecting and marketing efforts have to be ongoing, consistent and relentless. Hi Tech, Low Tech, no tech and sometimes shameless.

—Patricia Fripp

PROSPECTING AND marketing is a broad-brush term that can mean many things, and it is a method that can be accomplished in multiple different ways. Today, sales automation and digital marketing have begun to provide lead generation in exciting new ways. These developments certainly blur the line between these two critical functions.

This situation is a significant example of the need to adapt. Definitions at the heart of selling that were enough for decades no longer apply to the current landscape.

Going forward, we feel it is appropriate to blend prospecting and marketing together and even use the words interchangeably. For the sake of simplicity, we will refer to them as P&M.

For most of us offering financial services to the public, P&M is our biggest challenge and the hardest thing we do. Saying that P&M is our lifeblood is not an overstatement.

Here's our question:

If P&M is the lifeblood of your practice, how good are you at it?

For any established FSP, there should be only one answer to that question— "I am great at it"—but we seldom hear it. That's something FSN is destined to change for our students and members.

First the bad news. We may share some new ideas with you regarding P&M, but rest assured—there is still nothing easy about it.

Although we have struggled along with everyone else on this issue, as teachers we have studied the best practices of those who are exceptional at P&M. We have some good answers, but be forewarned, they aren't glamorous.

There is one thing that all good prospectors and marketers in all walks of financial services have in common, and it's mundane: they make prospecting and marketing their number one priority—not some of the time, but all the time, and by a wide margin. They think, eat, and breathe P&M. Every person they encounter, under every imaginable circumstance, is a prospect until proven otherwise.

P&M doesn't end until you do. It's ongoing. The better you are at marketing, the easier prospecting becomes. The two practices are inextricably linked.

With the advent of social media, new P&M opportunities appear almost daily.

P&M is a moving target throughout our career. It is also a different kind of challenge during the early years of our career, then during our peak years, and ultimately during our late career. The only comfort in P&M being our number one challenge is that if it weren't, we might not be as necessary to the process.

Let's look at the best practices we know of:

P&M is Powered by Relationship Building

Perhaps the most often heard axiom about P&M is that "it's all about relationship building." That's a completely true statement, but only if you're good at P&M. So, let's start our P&M discussion by taking a closer look at relationship marketing.

Building relationships with clients is at the very core of any P&M strategy. Referrals are, of course, the crown jewels, followed by centers of influence, prospecting nests, client appreciation events, and the like.

Also included in relationship building is *lifestyle marketing*. This includes things like community involvement; trade associations; charitable work; religious, ethnic, and political organizations; and of course various club memberships.

If you are good enough at most of the above to have all the prospects you need, move on to the next. If not, then read on.

If for no other reason, it is important to be exceptionally good at building relationships because it gives you a huge advantage over the intrusion technology focused on making you irrelevant.

So, what does it take?

One thing we're sure of: it isn't just about charm and personality. It's about one of our core beliefs that cannot be overemphasized:

> *Successful relationships are based upon those things that each party cannot easily get elsewhere.*

That statement is worth framing and hanging up on your wall. We give you permission to do so.

Think about every successful relationship you've had; that with your parents, your best friend, your spouse, your family members, your mentor, your first manager, your best clients, and so on. Regardless of what others may think of you, these individuals think you are special, and you think they are special too!

When it comes to navigating your way through the uncharted waters that lay ahead for our industry, our advice on relationships may be your most valuable takeaway from this guide. In fact, we predict that going forward, most FSPs will be going all in, regarding relationship building as a distinguishing characteristic of their practice.

FSPs must understand the difference between providing good service and staying in touch with customers and building lasting relationships with clients.

The latter is one of the few things left that intrusion technology cannot replace! That's why our above definition of successful relationships will be one of the keys to your indispensability.

How do we know?

The strength of your relationships will be the reason clients are willing to pay you fees—fees they will keep paying regardless of market fluctuations, interest rates, and other economic conditions.

That, in turn, will lead to them to do more and more business with you over their lifetimes. If you have the right relationship with them, we can guarantee this kind of experience. Here's another thing you can count on:

Relationship building is the linchpin to the upper and advanced markets.

Talk to anyone in financial services today, and you'll find that just about everyone has their sights on the same affluent professional or business owner. If you think this means the space for growing your future clientele is small, you're right. If you think your competition for the level of trusted adviser we train to handle this market is intense, you're dead wrong.

Yes, it's narrow, but its depth has yet to be measured. Let's face it:

> *What most FSPs say is their target market is exactly that: a target. It is not a reality.*

Successful relationship building is essential to work with the affluent, the prominent, the self-employed, the business owner, and the most financially independent prospects and clients. The farther up the socioeconomic ladder you go, the more that statement rings true.

When we say it is essential, we mean that in the upper markets, and agreement to pay a fee for services rendered to someone with whom the client has a relationship with is not only acceptable; it's preferred!

That fact is very important in your transition to charging fees, which is key to the FSN Client Acquisition Process, and to validating your indispensability to clients.

How do we know?

Look at the way successful business owners, successful professionals, and the affluent make decisions and undertake initiatives in other aspects of their lives:

- ➢ When they are committed to fitness, they hire a personal trainer.
- ➢ When health care is a priority, they have a concierge arrangement with their primary care physician.
- ➢ When they're careful about their diet, they pay a premium on everything they put into their mouth.
- ➢ When they build a new home, they hire an architect.
- ➢ When they take a vacation, they work with a personal travel agent.
- ➢ When their daughter gets married, they hire a wedding planner.

On the other hand, there are two things they don't do:

> ➤ When their son gets in trouble with the law, they don't get him a public defender!
> ➤ When they want financial advice, they don't go to the guy who sells IRAs at the strip mall!

For this category of prospect, when it comes to the big-ticket items in life, if it's a bargain, it's a mismatch. They'd rather pay a trusted and proven expert.

Now that we've defined what successful relationships are, we must address our concerns with most advisers. Many FSPs don't seem to have a clear handle on what meaningful relationships look like in their business or personal lives.

Trust us. You may think you do, but you likely do not.

Here are ten questions, your responses to which may help you gain some insight into your relationship-building skills.

1. When you start a relationship that you want to work, but it hits a bump in the road, are you usually successful at repairing it?
2. Have you had strong relationships in the past that you were not able to maintain over the long term?
3. Are your best friends people who have known you most of your life?
4. Have any significant relationships ended in conflict (divorces excluded)?
5. Can you quickly make a list of a half dozen or more people who, if you called them anytime, day or night, and told them you needed their immediate help, would drop what they were doing and come to your aid?
6. Think about your top five to ten clients (your criteria). Do they promptly return your calls?

7. If you asked your A-list clients to consider a tax strategy or private investment concept that you were highly confident about, but it required an upfront fee to you, what do you think your batting average would be?

8. If you changed broker dealers or operating platforms, would you hesitate because you were uncertain of your ability to move your top clients?

9. What percentage of clients have given you referrals who became clients?

10. How many of your clients ever invited you to attend a special personal event in their lives like a birthday, wedding, bar mitzvah, or Christmas party?

No matter what your answers, we hope you have more than a few clients who fit the profile of the last four questions.

Going forward, we suggest you try to envision the above questions as a rule of engagement when meeting with prospective clients. Here is some advice you are not likely to get elsewhere: in today's environment, if you don't see the potential for a trusting and lasting relationship, it is probably not worth your trouble to land a short-term customer.

Here's another simple litmus test. It is the uncompromising standard that legendary investor Warren Buffett applies to the CEO of any company that he considers investing in.

The Oracle of Omaha says, "Unless the answer to these three questions about the CEO is not only a yes, but a strong yes, none of the other considerations matter, because I will pass on the investment: (1) Do I like him or her? (2) Do I respect him or her? (3) Do I trust him or her?"

If you are confident that most of your A-list clients would also give you the nod on the same three questions, you probably are good at building relationships.

As previously mentioned, although we are rooting for

everyone, many of our readers may drop out by the time they finish this leg of our journey.

Our steadfast requirement is to make sure FSPs achieve a special place in the financial lives of their clients and, in many cases, even in their personal lives. You must be more than just someone your client bought a product from, although that's certainly a good start. You must be "their kind of person," someone they think of in a favorable light and with whom they feel they have a special relationship.

If such is not the case, then the following will be true:

> *You will struggle with our mandate of collecting fees, which, as we shall learn later, is the key to fending off both intrusion technology and the competition.*

Setting Some P&M Parameters

Remember the competition in the middle market and upper middle market comes from all directions, including, in some cases, our own product providers. They are reaching out to clients and prospects in every possible way, using every available medium, reminding them that institutions outlast people and they will always be there for your clients.

You must look at every other person or entity in contact with your client as a potential poacher. We've all dealt with this before, and most of us can handle it. Thanks to advances in communications, now, more than ever, we need to pay attention to this threat. Remember much of the same technology is available to us to counter these outreach efforts.

The bigger change was mentioned earlier—namely, the fact that clients will be paying a premium (in the form of your fee) to have you attached to the products they buy or the concepts they implement with you. What this means to you is that the smaller client may no longer be a practical option. By smaller client, we mean anyone who is not paying you enough on whatever it is you're offering them to be considered either significant or a good value.

Note: Significance and value are a function of two variables: volume and relationship. If the volume is big enough relative to your compensation, you're probably okay. Better yet, if the value of your presence in a client's life is big enough, the volume may not matter. In our view, that's what the future is all about!

It appears to us that the middle market that built the insurance, mutual fund, annuity, community bank, and financial planning industry is eventually going to be significantly diminished by online technology. Without analyzing what other markets are at risk, let's just move to the high ground. Let's talk about this: *the markets where the things that make you necessary never change!*

Since each FSP has a different practice, the sweet spot or market for our students cannot be defined objectively in this guide. What we do know is this: the greater the income, the more we can do for the prospect.

The minimum threshold we suggest is the long-standing Reg D requirement for private placements: *a minimum net worth of $1 million (not including residence) and/or a minimum adjusted gross income of $200,000.*

An important thing to remember is that, in terms of our future, income trumps assets every time. In our core market, taxes are usually a prospect's greatest expense. Today, that's usually tied to income.

We recommend $200,000 of AGI, because most of our marketing programs focus on business owners, medical professionals, and promising young talent. If their business is new but promising and not yet established, or if they are W-2 doctors with a hospital, their long-term potential probably makes them a good risk. Aside from doctors and other professionals, we feel the best market to focus on is the self-employed, specifically, business owners.

Here we recommend establishing your own minimum standards, but we urge you to aim high. You need to have a good batting average because, regardless of how you get in front of the business owner today, it will likely be costly in terms of money, time, or both.

Here's our universal marker: *The prospect must have income in excess of his or her lifestyle needs.*

Something especially daunting is that many FSPs spend a lot of money on lead-generation systems and other means of getting in front of their target prospects. All too often, that's where it ends. Once in front of the prospect, they don't know what to say or how to say it. More to the point, they don't know what to ask or how to ask it.

> *Proper discovery is our most important skill and,*
> *by far, the most difficult to master*

You can't afford to be just fair at discovery. You need to think of yourself as somewhere between very good and downright great at it!

So, after relationship-based P&M mastery, skillful discovery is our second mandatory requirement for the FSP of the future.

We take a deep dive into this subject in Chapters 6 and 7. For now, know that you cannot afford to lose a prospect because of poor discovery skills.

Once you get on sound footing and get to know the target prospects within your chosen market, you will want to work on finding effective ways to reach them. Now the real challenge of building a clientele begins: prospecting within your chosen market.

One thing we want to make clear: any strategy or tactic we discuss in this guide is one that one of us, or one of our close mentees, has had significant experience and success with.

We find that the best prospectors generally do one of three things very well:

> ➤ They invest significant resources in quality lead-generation services.
> ➤ They have a third-party relationship or platform that sponsors introductions.
> ➤ They are highly regarded specialists who do a lot of joint work.

Just about everyone else is a grinder. As we see it, the ugly truth about P&M is this:

> *Most approaches don't work all that well for the average producer.*

Even though we don't have any statistics to support our contention, we think the reason most P&M programs don't work all that well is because the results from similar methods vary dramatically from one FSP to another.

Two FSPs with similar credentials can use identical P&M programs and have very different results. For some, it works almost all the time. For others, it works for a while and then tapers off. For still others, it never gets off the ground.

Among the reasons that results vary, poor discovery skills are usually the chief one.

Now, let's look at three types of commonly known P&M programs with which we have had significant firsthand success:

Lead Generation Programs

Those who put significant resources into lead generation have made a conscious decision to reinvest a large part of their revenues in a P&M machine that mimics much of our industry itself.

It's not especially efficient, but it is effective.

One lead generator that we know will work is a telephone specialist calling from a quality source that provides qualified business owners with reasonable detail about the key metrics of their business. But it must be done right. The callers must be experienced callers who are scripted but don't sound like it, because the leads are expensive.

One of our highest-producing mentees hires retired agents from one of the career life companies in his area. He has a costly source for successful business owners, with enough detail for the caller to feel the lead is more like a referral. He pays his callers well and uses them until they burn out, which is usually within a year or two.

That sounds unkind, but that's the nature of the telephone solicitation business. Something important to know is that it is taxing work that takes a knowledgeable caller to secure qualified appointments. It demands combat pay, and like combat, it leads to fatigue and the need for regular breaks from the grind.

Of course, we hasten to add that you must follow the law on approaching individuals given "do not call" lists and so forth.

Does this method work?

Our protégé' is one of the ten longest-standing members of the Top of the Table in the world—thirty consecutive years and counting! He attributes his success to two things: his discipline with this and other prospecting systems and the mentors he chose. Both he and one of those mentors are available to FSN members.

Another producer, who is the mentor and personal coach to one of the authors (he's in his eighties), hires local college students to call law firms in his native Chicago. They talk to the managing partner about having the company's term insurance reviewed—all done by phone.

The pitch is quick and to the point. "We are a national firm specializing in term life insurance. We'd like to offer you a free quote on your existing term program. No obligation, just an assurance that you're getting your money's worth and that, if there's a better rate out there, we'll find it for you."

This simple approach has worked for him for over a dozen years. One reason is that he uses a little-known strategy that allows clients to get a deduction for term premiums paid to date, if they do a specialized type of exchange.

It goes without saying that since our mentor and his sons (partners) know their stuff, a lot of nice larger cases are opened by this process.

If you'd rather outsource, there are some credible lead-generation companies that will set up appointments with business owners and other market segments. We've used several and have a very short list of those that work.

Another of our closest associates (he brought one of the contributing authors into the business) outsources to a firm that charges an hourly rate, with no guarantees for appointments. They're good enough to do that!

Our friend has used them to supplement his activity for many years. The cost to him averages about $3,000 per month, which delivers between five and eight set appointments per month with qualified business owners. He has had a seven-digit income for the past decade, so this is only one source of his production. The fact that he stays with it year after year says it is a worthwhile investment.

Hybrid P&M

One of the most exciting things today are Web-based and digital marketing providers. This is a perfect example of the blurred line we've discussed between prospecting and marketing. These firms put together various types of campaigns to qualified databases that generate leads. Some even scrub the leads and set the appointments. We have a short list of vendors with whom we've had good results from this emerging marketing specialty. Each uses a different approach.

Some do professional-quality ads on local cable TV that are designed to gain responses by email or telephone. Others create digital marketing campaigns that promote a single concept or need by attaching a brief conversation between actors posing as ideal prospects and discussing a problem/need. Then their program passes hits on to the adviser. Still others offer media coverage in the form of radio and TV interviews.

One of the larger IMOs (independent marketing organization) or brokerage agencies we work with has taken marketing to a new level. They have a professional studio that advisers can use to shoot their own videos, advertisements, and taped interviews for local TV. They also have a very professional radio show format, designed for advisers to penetrate their local markets with a regular program focused on their special offerings. All of this is turnkey for our participating members.

This component of our business is growing so rapidly that we hesitate to cover too much of it in this guide. It is rapidly evolving even as we write these words. What we do know is that the thoughtful FSP should take a close look at the amazing tools offered by digital and media marketing.

Since most of these things tend to be expensive, we look at everything currently available and try to bring the best to our students. In the end, they decide what might work for them. Then, it either works or doesn't. Of course, win or lose, we report results to our participants and share these results throughout our network. Our job is to help FSPs get their best shot at a satisfactory result.

Sponsored Platforms

The second major lead generator for the producers we work with is sponsored platforms.

> As we all know, *how well we do on a first inter-view with a prospect can depend upon what door we walk in through.*

Sponsored platforms can vary, but the ideal is to be endorsed and introduced by a trusted adviser to the prospect. It may be as attractive as being housed in a property and casualty agency or being tightly aligned with a CPA firm or a law firm. All three of those situations may sound like a dream come true for many FSPs, but the devil is in the details.

Sponsored platforms only work if both parties know exactly what they're getting themselves into and if the expectations are realistic. That said, when sponsored platforms do work, they work very well. We think having a sponsoring platform will be an important strategy for successful FSPs going forward.

The better sponsored platforms almost always require a lot of "skin in the game" from the producer. When they don't, we become very skeptical. So, let's first talk about what doesn't work.

Beware of the bait and switch.

Many wholesalers, IMOs, and vendors in the marketplace claim to have the answer to various types of "strategic alliances." For most of us, they don't.

How do we know?

Because they are marketing their concept to the masses. By now, hopefully you know that sponsored marketing is all about the relationship and trust the adviser can establish with the P&C principal, CPA, banker, or other professional.

That is a slow and very personal proposition. It is also something we have learned must be done one relationship at a time and mostly behind closed doors.

Any potential platform sponsor has no interest in what you can do until they know who you are, until they know if they can trust you, and until they believe you can strengthen their relationships with their clients.

A feeling of comfort on those issues cannot be accomplished in classroom settings, reviewing ring binders and training you on how to talk to CPAs or other FSPs. If you need to be trained on how to talk intelligently with another financial professional, then sponsored marketing is probably not for you.

Here's the problem: *none of the platform programs that are promoted by broker dealers, wholesaling organizations, and marketing organizations lend themselves to scale.*

The idea that they can plug twenty-five FSPs paying a large fee into twenty-five willing CPAs seems absurd! We find it hard to understand why FSPs often fall for these pitches.

After these platform sponsors take your money, they want your business to go through their platform, while they keep promising the alliance will work over the long run. We know this from personal successful experience in teaming up with several sponsored platforms.

To use another simile: *Partnering with a third-party*

platform is like an organ transplant. You do one at a time, and without extreme compatibility, it seldom works.

The only reason any other financial services professional will align themselves with you will be because of you, not because you have been introduced to them by a third-party vendor!

Let's not confuse sponsored platforms with marketing programs that help the FSP improve on an existing CPA or attorney relationship by having the former accompany the latter to an informational learning event. In that case, we are helping the FSP without putting a target on the sponsors back. Using a group educational event can work very well in these situations.

More on this later.

Meanwhile, save your seminar money and invest in your own search, one candidate at a time. You'll have to kiss a lot of frogs, but it will be worth it over the long run!

Better yet, instead of focusing on just the CPAs whom everyone else seems to be after, consider other platforms. They can be almost any business owner who provides goods or services to other businesses, the affluent, or self-employed professionals. That's a long list if you think about it. All the prospect needs to do is agree to some mutually attractive form of ethical and compliant reciprocity.

One creative example of this came from one of our favorite megaproducers who lives in San Diego. Like many top producers, he has a fondness for expensive toys, so it was no surprise for us to learn he has a yacht at the San Diego Yacht Club.

He became friendly with the yacht broker who'd sold him his boat and created an arrangement whereby all other buyers from that yacht brokerage firm would be introduced to him. It has been a smashing success!

We know what you're thinking: Megaproducer, Southern California, and so on. He's probably one of those guys who just can't fail. The right breeding, connections, good looks, and charm. You need the whole package to run with the SoCal yachting circle.

The truth is—he came in the business after several years as a bartender in Las Vegas. He is a three-hundred-pounder who barely got out of high school, and the best thing we can say about his appearance is that he is "unfortunate-looking." (We have his permission to use that description, because he's very proud of what he's accomplished with it.)

You'd be right, however, about his not being able to fail.

> *The reason for his success is not because of advantages but because of disadvantages!*

In all the years we have known him, he has never changed his work ethic or his level of passion for our business.

In 2006, he walked across the stage to accept the trophy (from one of the authors) for being the number one agent in the largest life insurance company in the United States. On that occasion, his seventh consecutive year of winning the award, he had the same passion and work ethic he'd had on the day he stepped out from behind the bar and approached his first prospect. That's what it's all about!

Most of us know of similar stories. Whatever the sponsoring platform, virtually every highly successful FSP we know has strategic alliance or sponsoring platform. You need one too.

Note: Check with your compliance and oversight authorities on the right way to set up such arrangements. Remember that no matter how any significant economic benefit is passed on to a sponsoring platform, it must be appropriately licensed and qualified to receive compensation from an FSP.

Here's what many of us don't want to hear:

The key metric we have identified in most of the better lead-generation programs and sponsored platform providers is 50 percent.

Those FSPs who invest in programs that work spend approximately 50 percent of the commissions generated from those leads on the sourcing, appointment setting, or introductions.

The cost of the leads, the telephone solicitor, and the various expenses are almost always about 50 percent of commissions earned from the campaign. If the FSP has a sponsoring platform, the total cost is also usually the same.

And these are producers who are good at it!

We suggest our readers approach their P&M strategy with the 50 percent rule in mind. Remember this works best for those who can move the needle on prospects whom they've never met and yet who can successfully open cases on the first interview.

Most of us would agree that this is half our job. If it is, then giving up half our compensation for getting in front of enough of the right kind of people can be a bargain.

In the end, even the best of lead-generation programs and platform programs can only get you in the door. The rest is up to you.

Sorry, no magic sauce!

The Price of Success

We can further support the above argument about both lead-generation programs and sponsoring platforms by sharing a little-known fact—a fact that, although we cannot prove it empirically, we know to be essentially true.

Based upon our firsthand experience with the industry's

leading producers, *we estimate that as many as half of the Top of The Table members only receive about 50 percent of the commissions they generate. This is because the other half is paid to third parties like those described here.*

Mind you, that still leaves them enough to qualify them for the Top of the Table, so it must be working for them.

Just remember it probably takes an investment of about 50 percent of commissions earned from a program. There is no guarantee you will always get what you pay for, but the sponsored platform does work over the long run.

The Best Investment in P&M You Can Make

We have saved the best P&M strategy for last. There is one approach that doesn't suffer from the "doesn't work all that well" rule. Not in the least. In fact, when done properly, this one works just about all the time, and you won't have to invest any hard dollars. You still pay 50 percent of commissions generated, but you only pay on the actual sales made!

With this strategy, if there are no commissions, there are usually no significant expenses!

Guaranteed.

How do we know?

Like everything else we recommend in this guide, we've done it and done it successfully. In this case we've done it throughout our entire careers and are still doing it as a core part of our business and the FSN movement.

> *It's the forgotten art that combines* prospecting, marketing, and training, *so it's right out of our playbook.*

Joint Work

We warned you we weren't going to tell you anything you didn't already know. Before you skip to the next chapter, take a minute to review our philosophy on this, the best of all P&M tools—especially if you feel your best years lie ahead.

> *Joint work, the way we do it, can be a career changer for the right FSP!*

As discussed in the foregoing, if you use any of the vendors, strategic alliances, or lead-generation or sponsored platform programs all in, it will cost you about 50 percent of the commissions generated. If these things are worth a try, then joint work, our style, ought to be a no-brainer.

First, in most cases, the 50 percent of the case you give up to the right partner is the half of the case you never would have seen, let alone thought of.

Second, you cannot put a price on the value of working with an experienced and credentialed FSP. We have dozens of students who have invited us to help with cases. Many of them are million-dollar producers who know what they don't know. Or, if they once did know it, they've forgotten that they know it.

Our philosophy on joint work is another of the basic tenets of FSN.

At the behest of our members and students, it has become a major part of our offering at FSN. Our availability to qualified FSPs seeking our help is, of course, limited. That's why we are developing trained advocates to work with members.

What's exciting is that FSN has attracted several members who are excellent candidates to be on either side of a joint case.

It is important to note that our definition of joint work includes all financial service professionals. In addition to salespeople, there are CPAs, attorneys, bankers, and investment managers whom we do joint work with. We bring them in on our cases, and they bring us in on theirs. We even meet periodically to discuss new business development opportunities. Although these professionals never share their fees with us, and we seldom share our compensation with them, we consider the case work we do together to be joint work.

> *These partners within the FSN joint work family are "rainmakers" when they bring us cases and team members when we take them cases.*

This dynamic development is becoming one of the greatest benefits to members.

When we were young FSPs, joint work dramatically accelerated our rate of development. Now, we are very proud of what the joint work culture of FSN is providing our members. We are convinced that *joint work is the best P&M tool our sharing and caring industry offers.*

On the other hand, if a joint work culture isn't appealing to you, don't do any!

Like all our advice, we don't expect 100 percent buy-in from everyone.

We think the little verse below states our philosophy on joint work best. It was written almost one hundred years ago by a friend of the grandfather of one of the authors. It was written in Detroit, Michigan, where they both lived in the 1920s.

Like much of what we believe in, the message is one that never changes.

Sermons We See

I'd rather see a sermon than hear one any day
I'd rather one should walk with me than merely show the way

The eye's a better pupil and more willing than the ear
Fine counsel is confusing, but example's always clear
The best of all the preachers are the men who live their creeds
For to see the good in action is what everybody needs
And the lectures you deliver may be very wise and true
But I'd rather get my lesson by observing what you do

Edger A. Guest

Finally, we're not trying to be cryptic, but we do have a long-term solution for P&M, one that we help members of FSN master, but it's not a topic for this book. Yet it's no secret either. The greatest solution to the P&M problem is to have a reputation that proceeds you and emanates from an inventory of clients who not only are satisfied but also have become your advocates.

Frankly, this solution is not accessible to most FSPs. It takes not only planning and skill but also that uniquely human quality that, for now, remains beyond the reach of technology.

Again, this is something our students won't easily get elsewhere.

Rao-ism #67

No one succeeds alone—no one!

OPENING CASES

Ours is a simple business. It can be explained in a single sentence:

Getting in front of enough of the right kind of prospects under favorable conditions and, once there, knowing what to ask them and how to listen to them.

—Jack Kinder, legendary sales trainer and author

IT'S ALWAYS a great day in the life of an FSP when he or she opens a new case. Identifying the exact timing of this celebratory moment is a subject of debate.

For some, it's the casual meeting on the golf course or at a social event, when someone expresses enough interest in our work to agree to a meeting.

For others, a case is not declared opened until the discovery meeting has revealed an agreed-to problem and the fee for a feasibility study has been paid.

Like other steps in the FSN Sales Process, we see the point at which a case is opened as a matter of personal preference, so we are going to take a conservative approach that includes everyone. We're going to start at the very beginning.

Thus, part of what we're going to discuss is a continuation of the last chapter, specifically, prospecting and marketing.

For this discussion, the process of opening a case begins the minute you walk into the room to meet the prospect. This means that the first question we must ask is "What door did you walk in?" That leads to a second question: "How did you secure the appointment?"

To boil things down to the lowest common denominator, we are going to base our lesson on opening cases using the least attractive answers we can imagine to these two questions, as follows:

> ➢ Whichever door you walk in through, you do so as a complete and total stranger.
> ➢ The appointment was secured by direct mail and/or telephone.

If that's not enough of a handicap to prove we know how to open cases, we're going to go a step further by selecting prospects who are the two most upmarket and difficult to get in front of: doctors and successful business owners.

The first step we are going to look at is how to open a conversation that leads to the building of trust. We call this *the rhythm of opening cases.*

In the next chapter, we will cover the discovery process itself, which introduces *the language of engaging the prospect.*

Brad Etheridge on the Science and Art of Opening Cases

To examine techniques for opening cold cases, we turn to our partner Brad Etheridge. Brad has had huge success in the two most desirable markets we have worked in, doctors and business owners. In the pages to come, Brad shares his time-tested techniques for opening a case by using the oldest and most venerable door opener: direct mail. Again, we picked this because if you can grow your practice with doctors and business owners using direct mail, then other approaches should be easy!

If you're a bit skeptical about using direct mail in these two markets, you should be! We need to start with a hint as to why Brad's approach works. The three techniques we are about share with you are some of the most expensive ways of getting in front of the right kind of prospect that we are aware of.

Remember the 50 percent rule about P&M from the previous expenses? Here are three examples of it that have worked well for us.

For direct mail to work it must accomplish two things:

First, it must capture the subject's attention long enough for them to open and read whatever it is we send them.

Second, it must say something that arouses enough *interest* that they are willing to take a next step.

That said, for most doctors and business owners, those two achievements alone are not always enough.

You also often need a strong hook that will compel them to respond to your request for a meeting. Two of the three programs described below have that hook in spades!

Note: None of the three programs Brad is going to share were originated by any of us (although Brad has greatly enhanced them). They are the creation of highly successful FSPs who have generated millions in revenue using their respective marketing ideas. We have known them for many years and can attest to their results, which have helped them build a clientele of prominent doctors and business owners.

With that note in mind, consider that we have used these

three techniques many times and shared hundreds of thousands in commission dollars with the creators.

A few years ago, Brad coined a term for opening these kinds of cases: "softening the beachhead." He uses this reference because he knows you cannot walk through a less welcome door than direct mail, and you cannot be less familiar than a total stranger.

The objectives of Brad's case-opening techniques are, first, to gain enough trust with the prospect to begin a dialogue on personal issues, and second, to learn enough about the prospect to determine if there is reason for a detailed discovery meeting. If there is a reason to proceed, getting agreement to that meeting is never a problem for Brad. Below, he gives us some highlights:

Doctor Dinner Seminars

Our FSN members who are interested in the doctor market have exclusive access to a turnkey process ranging from mailing lists to seminar presentation materials. Every step of the process has been refined and perfected by me and my team, who have done hundreds of doctor-only seminars across the country. For those who qualify, one of the senior members of FSN is often available to present at the seminar. We recommend this step for those not used to this kind of marketing initiative, but as with all our offerings, the mechanics are up to the FSP.

Our purpose here is to talk about opening cases, so we'll start with how we set the stage. The details of the seminar are available to members, but what we want to share now is how to walk into a roomful of highly educated strangers and, before the evening is over, open some cases!

Touch Points of a Successful Doctor Workshop

The primary goal of the doctor workshop program is to create potentially profitable relationships between as many doctors as possible and the FSP hosting the event. What follows are some of the detailed mechanics of a well-planned event.

The first thing we do is size the market for the event in the local area the adviser has chosen. The adviser submits a request to us to measure the potential for a worthwhile turnout of qualified prospects. Our target is doctors within a thirty-mile radius of the venue.

We look for a minimum of twenty-five hundred physicians and dentists. To be sure we have the best information, we use one of three recognized providers of market data. These services also prepare and deliver the invitations and gather the RSVPs as they are received. Assuming that there are enough doctors in the area, we secure the venue for the event sixty days prior to the workshop.

The venue must have room to seat forty comfortably. Although we like well-known white-tablecloth venues such as Ruth's Chris or Morton's, the most important thing the venue must provide is flexibility. We must have the service captain agree to follow our instructions in detail, including the timing of course service and the serving of alcohol, coffee, and especially dessert, which should be cold and laid out ahead of time so as not to interrupt our presentation. These events are expensive and only work well when every detail is planned.

When you are dealing with doctors who have usually put in a long and demanding day, you know their attention span may be limited. You must be efficient with the use of their time.

On the day of the event, we meet with the restaurant staff and review everything again. Most advisers have done plenty of seminars, but when it comes to doctors, it's a different ball game. It's a real science!

After attending to the many details that go into getting doctors to show up to an event, the real work begins when they arrive.

The presenter delivers a presentation that consists of thirty-eight slides. This is proprietary to our members, as it took years of trial and error for us to perfect.

The last thing done upon conclusion of the presentation is the completion and gathering of workshop contact forms. These forms are designed to assist us in determining how we follow up with the doctor. It allows the doctor to request additional information on the items covered in the presentation, and it provides us with contract information.

Upon completion of the contact forms, the presenter tells the audience that he will remain to answer questions until the last doctor leaves.

This all sounds rather routine, but it is anything but that. If ever there was a case of the devil being in the details, this is one. There are three things we do that make our doctor seminars a success, where so many others have failed:

- ➢ First is the specialized detail referred to above that gets the doctors to the event and ensures that they will have an enjoyable and informative evening. We never get negative feedback at the end of a session.
- ➢ The presentation itself is an eye-opening series of issues, problems, and opportunities that is customized to the life experience of doctors.
- ➢ Finally, the Q&A period at the end of the presentation is when the presenter establishes rapport and demonstrates a thorough understanding of the circumstances unique to doctors.

All of this leads to a very high number of requests for appointments with the hosting FSP (over 50 percent). FSN has the only successful turnkey program for opening the doctor market that we are aware of.

We do not recommend this market to novices, unless they are working jointly with a knowledgeable adviser. Doctors are as difficult to work with as they are valuable!

For those who are ready, FSN has a turnkey approach to one of the most lucrative markets anywhere!

Business Owners

As we've mentioned, our experience with business owners has extended throughout our entire careers. We are going to share the most innovative approach we know of, and then one of the most common.

The first has earned its creator millions of dollars. We've done well with it too! So, let's start there.

Note: We must caution the reader that this approach to prospecting is very expensive.

Except for the fact it works.

For it to work, however, requires a very well-scrubbed mailing list that includes detail about the business owners' net worth, company revenues, and company ratings. Additional information, like form 5500 on their existing qualified plan from the IRS and related details, is also needed. These are prospects who, when they buy, buy big!

The approach is known by insiders as "the Box."

The client receives via FedEx a Tiffany-style box, beautifully wrapped, with a letter that says some proprietary things that get the recipient's attention.

While we won't share the letter in its entirety, we will share the most important line of the letter: "Enclosed are one hundred reasons why business owners like you have benefited immensely by meeting with my firm."

> *In the box are one hundred newly printed one-dollar bills!*

What is said to get past gatekeepers and others for a solid appointment is also proprietary. What matters for our purposes is what we do when we receive word of a confirmed appointment.

The second approach to getting in front of business owners is more traditional and should be considered by those with no natural access to this market. The leads are purchased from a lead-generation service. We provide the service with a description of what we do and who we are looking for, usually things like executive benefits or retirement plans exclusively for the owner and key employees. Of course, when there's a better attention-getter, like new tax laws, we focus on that.

You can pay a lot or a little to get in front of a business owner.

Here's a surprise: *you pretty much get what you pay for!*

That said, this is about opening cases, and we believe the process for that is the same.

Most producers make the mistake of going into this kind of call with the preconceived notion that they must impress the prospect with their credentials—years in the business, education, designations, what their firm does for business owners, and so forth.

That's another place where we depart from conventional approaches.

> *The prospect doesn't care what you know until he knows that you care!*

We don't believe in small talk on this kind of lead. The prospect often doesn't even remember why he accepted the appointment. So, we get right to the point. First, we let him know that anything he shares with us is completely confidential and that in twenty to thirty minutes it will be clear to both of us if we need to meet again. There will be no further meetings unless the prospect requests one.

Here's the difference in our process from most other sales approaches:

We do our homework prior to the appointment.

We go on the Web and research the prospect as deeply as possible. We start with the history of the company he owns, any press or articles, any awards won—that is, how the company grew after he took it over when Dad died. But we don't stop there!

If you dig enough, you can find news items that quote the prospect, cite his kids' high school sports achievements, or presents his parents' obituaries—anything you can use to get the conversation started and let the prospect know you took the time to learn a little about him. However, don't dig too deep. Prospects don't want to be reminded of a bankruptcy or divorce!

Lead off early in the discussion with a carefully crafted question that serves as what we call an icebreaker: "I'm impressed with your 300 percent sales growth over the past five years, so I'd like to ask you a personal question if I may. How does a political science major do so well running a precision aircraft parts company?" (This was a real question that helped flip an ice-cold call into a longtime and valued client.)

The answer is almost always the same. "How the heck did you know that?"

"I like to do my homework and be sure of who I'm talking to." This shows respect.

Then follow up with a softball like, "How did you decide to get into this kind of business?" We promise that this kind of question will get you as much as twenty minutes of listening time, during which the prospect will find you fascinating!

Once the prospect stops to catch his breath, we spend just two or three minutes telling him who we are and what we do for business owners (you'll learn lots of one-liners at our FSN events).

Next, to segue into the essence of the meeting, we ask our favorite question:

> *"When you wake up at three o'clock in the morn- ing and you're staring at the celling thinking about the business, what keeps you awake?"*

Regardless of the answer—and the prospect will always answer if you press him—it's critical not to think about a solu- tion. Our closing line is always: "That's an interesting concern. I have a couple of ideas I'd like to research based upon your unique circumstances. I'll bet I can even give you an idea or two that may help you get back to sleep. Mr. Prospect, it seems to me we have a pretty good reason to meet again. Will that work for you?"

The answer is almost always a yes, but the key development here is that we have not even hinted at a solution!

Two keys to a successful meeting are what we call tracking and touring.

We have learned to track the prospect during the interview, or as professional poker players say, to "look for tells." We al- ways ask for permission to take notes, and then when we do, it's not just the notes we write down that we are interested in. It's how the prospect answers, how he processes information and communicates. We especially listen for words he uses to describe his situation. Whenever possible, we want to use those same words when we come back for our next meeting.

> Before leaving, *we always make the prospect an offer he can't refuse. We ask him for a tour of the company.*

Usually, we don't even have to ask. Either way, that tour will take you a long way down the garden path toward winning a new client. Prospects love showing us their life's work, and they treat us like they would a prospective employee or a banker from whom they want to get a loan.

These are the relationship builders that cannot be picked up by technology. It's the stuff that makes you indispensable. Buy the way, joint work with a pro in these markets is the fastest way to pick up these skills. As we like to say, *the best skills in selling are caught, not taught!*

We've mentioned that, although the FSN Client Acquisition Process is specific and disciplined, the lines of distinction are sometimes blurred. One example is the difference between prospecting and marketing discussed in chapter 4. Another is the point at which the discovery process begins.

In the foregoing examples, discovery can sometimes be handled in the first interview. Other times, especially in more complicated situations, it requires a second and much more lengthy meeting.

The key is this:

You never *take shortcuts on the discovery process.*

Throughout this guide, we have repeatedly emphasized that none of what we ask of our students is going to be easy. If you're going to be a factor in our market, even those things that come naturally for some of us need to be put into high gear. If there's a takeaway for our readers, we hope it is this:

The secret to success is that there is no secret!

What Fifteen Years of Working with Doctors Has Taught Me about My Profession

In our authors' notes at the front of this guide, we mentioned that we use comparisons to doctors throughout this guide for very good reasons.

There is no professional we in financial services like to compare ourselves to more than medical doctors. For the authors, this is especially true. We have worked with literally thousands of doctors over the decades and conducted hundreds of doctor seminars for planning purposes. One of us is even married to a physician!

Although this guide is full of comparisons to doctors, for the most part, we may be flattering ourselves. Still, we can't overlook the similarities.

They have us on things like the difference between our respective definitions of quality of life. We concede who does the more impactful work.

Another comparison they win big on is what doctors must achieve in the way of education and experience. Think of what they must accomplish before they're even allowed to pick up a stethoscope, let alone a scalpel!

Conversely, consider what must we achieve before we pick up a pen and say, "Sign here, here, and here."

Still, there are striking similarities.

We think one of the least recognized is the one most

important to this guide. We see the leading personality patterns in the medical profession as being very similar to ours.

In our experience, working with thousands in both professions, we've noticed that most tend to fall into one of three broad categories.

Let's look at medicine and allow the readers to identify the similarities with financial advisers for themselves.

The first are those doctors who are the scientists. Their passion is analytics and problem solving. The scientists are usually specialists.

It seems to us that the more brilliant they are, the narrower their area of specialization is– and the greater their income.

The second group goes into medicine because of the humanitarian factor. They have a passion for helping others and usually have great people skills. Doctors without Borders comes to mind first, but you don't have to go to Africa or India to find these healers. Many are the local internist who has a great and caring bedside manner.

The third category is the person who goes into medicine for the socioeconomic status. We have spent more than our fair share of time with Beverly Hills cosmetic surgeons, dermatologists, stomach staplers, and related personal enhancement physicians. They do well for, and are paid well *by*, the upper-income market they serve.

As FSPs, we believe you too must be a specialist, a specialist who cultivates all three characteristics discussed above: a fascination with discovery, compassion for your client, and the ability to demand a premium for your specialized services.

It's not hard to see that the relative seriousness and complexity of an illness correlates with the degree of specialization needed to treat it. That doesn't diminish the role of the general practitioner, who can handle most minor ailments and even some chronic ones with the same patient. All the same:

The more that's at stake, the more we want to seek the advice and care of a specialist. And, yes, the more we trust that the specialist will solve our problem, the more we are willing to pay.

In medicine, the specialist informs the other caregivers about her plan of treatment and discusses how it may impact other aspects of the patient's overall health. Here's where we differ:

Doctors don't invite other caregivers to bless or second-guess their treatment plan.

At FSN, we agree with the way doctors do things. We encourage FSPs to identify a few strategies that can be highly valuable to their market and then become best in class at those few things.

Do it right, and do it with competence and passion. If you follow this advice, then prospects may trust and respect you before they even meet you!

Rao-ism #75

The difference between the right word and al-most the right word is the difference between lightning and a lightning bug.

Discovery, a Key to Your Indispensability

It was within the words he didn't speak, that I found the answers to my questions.

—Alfa H., philosopher and poet

SKILLFUL DISCOVERY is the centerpiece of the FSN Client Acquisition Process. Without it, indispensability is an impossibility.

If we can recover the best from our past and create a version of ourselves for the future that cannot be converted to robotics, it will be the discovery process that holds the key. Here's why:

We sell by asking questions, while remembering that no one ever lost a sale by listening too much.

Yet discovery has long been undertrained and misunderstood by most of our industry. In the environment we see on the horizon, discovery will be, hands down, the most important part of a compliantly conducted sales process.

Discovery begins by getting to know your prospects and getting inside their heads and their hearts in a good way. It continues until an agreed-to problem is discovered (or not). Then, it concludes by showing prospects how their personal values hold the key to our being able to help them.

> *Discovery is the prospect's reason for doing business with you.*

Ask any trial lawyer what the most important thing is in winning a case. Without missing a beat, they will tell you that it is discovery.

Ask any physician what the most important part of successful medical treatment is. The answer is always an accurate diagnosis.

Here's our question:

> *If you agree that skillful discovery is at the heart of a successful sales process, how good are you at it?*

By our admittedly stringent standards, we feel that the majority of FSPs are somewhere between mediocre and terrible at this most vital of skills.

Sadly, in many cases, discovery is an engineered groove that product pushers and single-solution promoters manipulate the prospect to accept as something of "unique value."

In such cases, it's usually a predetermined product or concept, which is what makes this kind of sales process disingenuous. We believe that going forward, many FSPs who probably see themselves as ethical may find themselves on the wrong side of a suitability dispute.

When a consumer decides to invest in a financial product or strategic concept without a clear understanding of why he made the decision to do so, it can lead to problems later. Over time, and in the right forensic hands, the result can be catastrophic for the FSP.

Our approach to discovery involves a series of steps that lead us, not the prospect, down a path, an uncharted path that the prospect shows us while often learning of it for the first time herself.

Discovery is about getting responses to skillfully asked questions. We say responses because often they are not specific answers. Sometimes they're just questions back at us, or statements that help guide the conversation in a different direction.

As we proceed with our tutorial on discovery, we ask that the reader accept another of our seeming non sequiturs:

➢ Questions are not what you must master in discovery.
➢ It's all about skillful listening to responses that may lead to another question and yet another.
➢ Eventually, the prospect will tell you how to make a client of her.

The notion of conducting an effective discovery interview is nothing new.

The pivotal importance we place on it may be new to most readers. The market we have outlined as a goal for our students and the purview of the FSPs we work with can best be successfully penetrated by those who are not just good at discovery but among the best.

How do we know?

For most of the FSPs we work with, even top producers, mastering discovery is their highest entry barrier to the advanced markets. Once this is conquered, they have a distinct advantage over their competition. More importantly, they find that the traditional challenges in relationship building are greatly diminished.

Crossover

In our review of the earliest sales training, we noted that it consists of a series of steps. Each one could be viewed as a "sale within a sale" or, in more contemporary terms, a benchmark. The discovery process contains more subtle steps, but for our purposes here, they too are benchmarks.

Let's look at the most important of these markers.

The FSN Client Acquisition Process identifies the key benchmark as the *crossover point*. Crossover is the point during the discovery meeting when the prospect has made two important decisions:

➤ First, that you are competent.
➤ Second, that you are trustworthy.

In our view, both things should occur routinely, and in that order.

> *Competence is established when you help the prospect shine a light on a significant problem she didn't know she had, or if she does know of it, she doesn't know what to do about it.*
>
> *Trust is accomplished when the prospect realizes that you are a creditable choice for proposing possible solutions to an agreed-to problem.*

When competence and trust are established, the client relationship begins, and the wind is at the FSP's back!

At this point, prospects will usually agree to pay an initial fee for a feasibility study. Without it, the acquisition of a client is far less likely.

Get these three things done, and both you and the prospect have *crossed over* in the relationship to full engagement.

At this point, the step from engagement to client is usually the FSP's to lose. It all comes together quite seamlessly.

There's another reason for the fee: objectivity.

The choice of a solution will ultimately be up to prospect. This reality is why we built the Decision Process software, covered in Chapter 8.

For those not accustomed to asking for fees, some additional training may be required. We offer help with this at our FSN training events. There is also significant literature on the subject through most compliance and marketing platforms.

What you choose to call your fee is a personal issue and may depend upon the compliance and oversight rules that you adhere to in your practice.

The key is that you conclude every discovery meeting that results in a legitimate prospect for your services by offering a feasibility study as the next step. Get this done, and you've *crossed over* the traditional line of sales resistance to competence and trust. What this means to you is that you are now *the FSP of choice to work on a problem that the prospect has identified with your help.*

If you position yourself correctly, no one else is going to be brought in to review your work. The prospect has already identified and paid for an expert opinion.

For most, the toughest thing about discovery is the discipline of sticking with the process no matter what!

Ironically, some of our most experienced and successful students are so good at opening relationships with prospects that they have trouble moving through the discovery phase at a disciplined pace. With this level of FSP, most failures to convert qualified prospects to clients are almost always the result of poor discovery.

How do we know?

All we need do is to review the way in which the adviser

made the decision about what to recommend to the prospect. The problem is that the adviser often knows (or thinks she knows) what the likely recommendation will be.

What we see repeatedly with highly qualified FSPs is that this light bulb may go on in their minds long before the client has come to terms with the possibility that there even is a problem.

As specialists, we make our livings by dealing with a handful of problems with which we are intimately familiar. Should it be any surprise if we have an idea of possible problems before the discovery process shines a light on them?

Once again, we need only to look to our doctor friends. After they examine and interview their patients, do you think most competent doctors have a pretty good idea of a typical patient's problem? You bet they do!

Would you like your doctor to jump on a treatment program before getting the lab results he would typically order before moving forward?

Of course, the liability alone negates that possibility, not to mention that *a rushed diagnosis is an invitation to seek another opinion.*

We should never proceed in such a fashion for the same two reasons.

FSPs often forget that their recognition of the problem is not the purpose of discovery. Only the unique version of that problem, as it is seen through the eyes of the prospect, matters. (The careful reader will recall our little verse from Chapter 2.)

> *We call this epiphany by the prospect a "realization." And mastery of its discovery, along with the prospect, is nothing less than the essence of your craft.*

Ironically, the goal of our Client Acquisition Process is

to have prospects tell you what you may already know—and what they may already know too. They just didn't know they knew it!

This is a huge point. The most important aspect of discovery is not what the adviser discovers but what the prospects discovers by themselves.

Rao-ism #82

What we think of as the moment of discovery is really the discovery of the right question.

A LESSON FROM A MASTER OF DISCOVERY

What's important about money to you?

—master of discovery and values-based selling coach
Bill Bachrach

NOW WE are going to demonstrate why discovery is the one thing that we can guarantee will be immune to intrusion technology. We are going to take a deep dive into the art and science of discovery with another of our partners, George Thom.

George has developed and refined the art of discovery for over forty years. He has taught it to salespeople throughout North America.

The Discovery Process guide is a composite from the works of the originators of discovery in the life insurance industry. They include Tom Wolff, Dick Sikorsky, Jim Jacobs, Simon Singer, Rao Garuda, and Bill Bachrach.

What follows is a combination of their teachings, along with our own input. George ties it all together, simultaneously providing a large number of his own verbal gems.

Note: Neither George nor the other authors claim any exclusivity to the art of discovery. We do claim unquestionable authority in its execution, which we will now pass on to the readers for their consideration.

In short, we didn't make the Stradivarius, but we can play it as well as anyone in the world!

The Discovery Process According to George Thom

We like to compare the discovery process to a tree because our prospects' responses take us to new branches to explore. Having said that, we only follow the tree analogy minimally, so we don't lose that which is important in trying to fit material to the tree.

The Discovery Process is built on the skillful use of questions.

You already ask questions. You already probe, disturb, and look for what we once called "hot buttons."

What is different here is that our goal is to raise your level of consciousness and provide you and the prospect with multiple aha moments that occur when anyone experiences realizations for the first time.

One thing all the sections of the Discovery Process have in common is that they employ something we call the Power Combination.

The Power Combination—Realization and Values

In 2005, the internet featured a video of two men in white lab coats dropping Mentos mints into two-liter bottles of Diet Coke. This resulted in impressive foamy geysers, and the videos soon went viral.

Science teachers had dropped vinegar into baking soda decades earlier to set off reactions, but the Mentos and Diet Coke experiment was the one that caught the world's attention. By themselves, Mentos sit quietly in their package or in a bowl, and a glass of Diet Coke appears totally innocent. However, combining them creates a powerful reaction.

The questions we ask our prospects may seem routine, but what many FSPs fail to realize is that if we combine these questions properly, we can set off a reaction that changes everything.

In Simon Singer and Rao Garuda's classic pamphlet "Eleven Most Powerful Questions," question one is "What is your largest expense?"

Many of us have asked that question, and by itself, it frequently opens the door to our being "invited in" by the client. But most of us fail to see two things.

First, we fail to see that this is an affirmation question. The prospect will see taxes in a different light for the first time.

Let's look at that question again:

What is your largest expense?

Most prospects answer it wrong. They say things like housing, entertainment, education, and the like. It is only upon reflection that they have an aha moment when they realize, for the first time, that their largest single expense is taxes.

The next step requires timing. At the right moment, we need to ask what sales coach Bill Bachrach calls a *values* question. For example, "What would it mean to your family if we could reduce your tax bill?"

The Power Combination is the proper coordination of realization questions and values questions

First, ask a *realization* question.

The client has never thought about taxes as being his single largest expense. This realization can sometimes almost be an epiphany.

Pause, and let that sink in for a moment.

Next, ask a *values* question.

"What would it mean to your family if we could reduce your tax bill?"

This one-two effect is what gives the Power Combination its potency. We will furnish you with several examples of both questions in the coming pages, but first, let's look at two *real-life examples from our case files*:

Example #1. An attorney recently attended his first FSN Summit. He had built his career on "rainmakers" from the financial community but wanted to interest prospective clients to call him. He soon reported that he had a significant breakthrough using these principles. He was asked by a new acquaintance, "What do you do for a living?"

He responded, "I help people reduce their largest single expense."

"Oh? And what would that be?"

"What do you think it is?"

Within a few seconds, the prospect said, *"It's taxes, isn't it?"*

The attorney nodded his head and let that sink in.

The prospective client said, "I have never thought about it like that."

The attorney then asked a values question: "How would it impact your life if we were to reduce your tax bill significantly?"

The prospect answered at great length, talking about sending his kids to college, retiring early, and just having some extra disposable income. The two exchanged cards and arranged a meeting.

Example #2. To show the *adaptability* of these techniques, let's step out of our financial services box.

A Florida woman missed her daughter and grandson, who were living in upstate New York. She wanted to persuade them to move to Florida. She met an FSN member who suggested she try the Power Combination.

Her son-in-law was a materials fabricator, and his industry was vanishing from his region of the country. The FSN member suggested she ask a *realization* question and follow it up with a *values* question.

She asked her son-in-law, "How old do you want to be when you realize that you have to change careers? Did you know that your skills are transferrable to the manufacturing and repairing of boats?"

She followed that up with a values question:

"What would it mean to you if you knew your future employment was secure?"

Then, she spoke with her daughter, whose son, Billy, was prone to asthma attacks in the winter.

"Wouldn't Billy's asthma be improved if he grew up in a warm environment?"

Then, she asked a values question:

"How important would it be to you as a mother to know you have done everything within your power to keep your family healthy?"

This combination of *realization* and *values* questions is the key.

And using them will change your career.

And your life.

Questions That Secure the Appointment

We might say we are now at the bottom of the tree that we wish to ascend.

The first step is securing the appointment.

The following is taken from an FSN Summit. Please note his use of realization questions, highlighted in **bold**, and *values* questions, set in *italics*.

We usually spend a lot of time talking about taxes with prospects.

What part of reducing your taxes is of interest to you?

Is it about having a business entity that would allow you to take deductions that you couldn't take under a different type of entity?

Is it about being able to produce tax-free income?

Is it about being able to make more efficient contributions to your retirement plan?

The prospect may say, "I'd be interested in ..." (*Note:* This can be anything.)

Say the prospect responds this way: "I'd be interested in saving some taxes on my discretionary income."

Tell me why that would be an issue of interest to you. Tell me how that might make a difference in your life.

Would it enable you to retire earlier?

Would it enable you to fund your children's education in a more efficient manner?

Would you to be able to give more money to charity?

Would you to be able to enhance your lifestyle?

"I think we are going to be able to help you, but we can only do it with your full cooperation. Frankly, neither you nor I have the time to play around with this, so one of the things I want to be certain of is that you are going to give us your cooperation in total. If not, then it's been nice meeting you, but maybe this isn't the right time for you."

Look back at the questions highlighted. They are realization questions. The prospect has likely never given serious thought to reducing her taxes. These questions awaken something within her that makes her realize that she can do something to reduce her taxes.

The first question seems innocuous enough: **What part of reducing your taxes is of interest to you?**

This question by itself may not deliver a motivated prospect, but when taken with the follow-up questions, it will likely ignite a spark.

Is it about having a business entity that would allow you to take deductions that you couldn't take under a different type of entity?

If this gets attention, expand on the subject.

Is it about being able to produce tax-free income?

The odds are in your favor because your prospect would certainly like to produce tax-free income but doesn't know how to do it.

Is it about being able to make more efficient contributions to your retirement plan?

> Now, you will have her undivided attention.
> At this point, values questions come into play.
> Let's look at them again:
> Would it enable you to retire earlier?
>
> ➢ Would it enable you to fund your children's education in a more efficient manner?
> ➢ Would it enable you to give more money to charity?
> ➢ Would it enable you to improve your lifestyle?

Getting the prospect to vocalize how you could change her life is crucial. The interview process is transformed from trying to persuade your prospect to do something she isn't motivated to do to giving her something she realizes she sincerely wants.

That is powerful.

The Discovery Process is about changing the interview process from being a contest of wills and wits to awakening something within the prospect that is values driven.

Once more, this is powerful.

This alone is enough ammunition to enhance the coachable reader's practice. But we've got more to share with you, all from real cases we have worked on.

Questions That Motivate

There have been numerous studies of great athletes to determine just what it is that enables them to perform at high levels. Slow-motion photography can break down the golf swing, the baseball swing, and the basketball jump shot. But, as helpful as these studies may be, the novice most likely can never get beyond a certain skill level because of physical limitations. Even the greatest athletes find that their physical prowess diminishes over time.

That is where the FSP has some great advantages. Our skills improve over time and remain with us decades after athletes are forced to the sidelines. In addition, studying our great performers can enable us to produce at extremely high levels.

What we believe makes our approach to discovery exceptionally valuable is that it identifies, for the first time, the Power Combination, that is, the use of realization questions and values questions.

The Power Combination—Realization and Values Questions

Think of a game of volleyball. A player in the back ranks hits the ball to a player up front. That player sets up the spike, and a third teammate slams the ball over the net into the ground.

That setup and spike is transferrable to the Power Combination. It is quite simple, and once you understand it, you can use it with ease. Most importantly, you do not need sales skills equivalent to those of the world-class athlete.

Let's look at some motivating questions.

Perhaps the best examples of motivating questions are the Eleven Most Powerful Questions, below.

Again, the realization questions are in **bold**, and the *values* questions are in *italics*.

The Eleven Most Powerful Questions

By Rao Garuda and Simon Singer

Question 1: ***What is your largest expense?*** Wait. If necessary, ask, "What about taxes? Wouldn't that be a large expense?"

"If you were able to reduce your taxes, would that be something of significant help?"

Question 2: **"What have you done to create tax-free income for your retirement?"**

"When you reach age seventy and a half, you are going to need to take mandatory distributions from your retirement plan."

"Are you aware that you are going to be taxed on that money?"

"What I am suggesting is that there are ways, statutory, in the tax code, to be able to turn that into tax-free income.

"How would that impact your life?"

Question 3: **"How much of these retirement accounts are yours?"**

Think about every financial statement you have ever seen. It shows the person's income and the person's expenses. It shows the individual's assets and liabilities. But when you get to *the person's retirement account, it only shows the gross number.*

So, if the retirement account shows $1 million, that $1 million is not real. There is a liability against it. That lien is called federal, state, and local income taxes—and possibly even estate taxes.

"Are you telling me I don't have to pay taxes on that money?"

"Well, right now, you don't really have a million

dollars in there that you can spend. You have anywhere from five hundred thousand to six hundred thousand spendable dollars.

"Would it be of interest if we could figure out some ways that would allow you to spend the entire the entire one million, as opposed to six hundred thousand?"

Question 4. **"Did you know you can have guaranteed income for life?"**

What would it mean to you to know that you could never outlive your income?"

Question 5: **"Did you know that estate and capital gains taxes are voluntary?**

How would your family feel if they knew that everything you own will stay in the family, as opposed to going to lawyers, probate expenses, and the IRS?"

Question 6: **"What have you done to protect yourself from lawsuits, liens, and judgments?"**

Typical answers include liability insurance and umbrella coverage. Even the most sophisticated prospects are often clueless about asset protection.

"Did you know that every one of those has limits?

"The government taxes what you own; it does not tax what you control.

"People can sue successfully against what you own. They can't sue successfully against what you control.

"So, in a perfect world, you own as little as possible and you control as much as possible.

"Do you have children?"

"Are they married?" "Are they planning to get married?"

"If they get married, is there a chance they could get divorced?"

"Did you know that the protection against lawsuits, liens, and judgments also flows over to your children and your grandchildren, to make certain that the assets stay in the bloodline that you created?"

"Would that be of any interest?"

"What would that mean to you?"

Question 7: **"Did you know you could insure your IRA / profit sharing plan?"**

"When you start taking distributions, they are potentially available to creditors and lawsuits. We may be able to protect you from that."

"How might that help your life?"

Question 8: **"Do you have the cash to pay the taxes on your IRA / profit sharing plan?"**

"If you take $100,000 distribution from your retirement account, at your tax bracket, you are going to have send $40,000 to the Internal Revenue Service to pay the tax."

"Where is that money going to come from?"

"If there were a way you didn't have to write that check to the IRS, how might that affect your decision about withdrawals from your IRA?"

Question 9: **"Did you know the IRS will give you a tax deduction today for a charitable gift that you do not make until after you and your spouse pass away?"**

"How could those tax deductions impact your life?"

Question 10: **"Have you ever lost money in the stock market?"**

"Would you sleep better at night if you knew you were able make an investment that tracks with the stock market but guarantees you will never lose any money?"

Question 11: **"Did you know there are processes available that will pay you tax-free income if you live too long, die too soon, or need long-term-care coverage?"**

"What would that mean to you and your family if you could eliminate those worries?"

Some of the preceding questions can arguably be categorized as both realization questions and values questions, but our intent is to raise your awareness level.

What matters is that these questions certainly motivate, and that is the theme of this section.

Questions That Reveal Values

The book *Values-Based Financial Planning* by Bill Bachrach is a great resource for anyone in financial services who deals with the public.

Let's look at some of his recommendations.

Ask the following questions:

"What's important about money to you?"

And wait for the answer. Let the prospect tell you what is important to him or her.

And follow up on each answer with another question:

"Why is that important to you?"

Bill uses the analogy of ascending a staircase, but we don't think he would object to our use of a tree analogy, in which one answer leads to the next question.

If there is a pattern to these questions, it is asking, "What is important about …?"

By using this method of questioning, you will learn more about the client than you ever thought possible.

Let's look at three actual cases of ours that went from failure to success because the FSP had an understanding of the client's values.

Note: Some of the topics and language in this section may be new to you or beyond your area of comfort. The only issue is, Do you have prospects or clients who may be candidates for the items discussed? And if not, would you like to? That's what our view on joint work at FSN is all about. We have members who can help on these kinds of cases *until you are good enough to help others in the same way.*

Example 1

The clients were interested in setting up a charitable

foundation to benefit some local organizations but were hesitant to go forward.

A series of gently asked discovery questions uncovered the key issue.

The local organizations were run by people who weren't particularly nice to their daughter. The daughter, evidently, was not "stylish" enough to suit them, so although the clients supported the work of the organizations, they were reluctant to fund them because of this issue.

The solution was to make the daughter the chair of the Donor Committee. The snooty organization leaders quickly learned to be courteous and respectful. It even gets better. As the daughter got to know these people, genuine friendships developed, and it truly became win-win.

Example 2

The client was not charitably inclined.

Questioning revealed that the client was not interested in donating to a church, school, or hospital. What he liked to do was hunt elk.

The solution was to establish an elk preservation fund to preserve the herd. He was later recognized by the governor of his state and has become an active conservationist who continues to hunt elk to this day.

Example 3

This client was almost identical in his values as the elk hunter, except that his passion was sailfish.

Here are the questions asked:

➢ "Is your sailfish passion expensive?"
➢ "Did you know we could make it tax-deductible?"
➢ "What impact would that have on your life if we were to do that?"

A foundation was established and exists to this day. The client tags the sailfish and sends the data up to satellites, enabling universities around the world to study the migration habits of sailfish.

Values questions are limitless.

The more we understand our clients, the better we can serve them. And the more they will want to do business with us.

Questions That Disturb

This section may be controversial to some of our readers, so it is presented without persuasion.

There are times in the discovery interview when we are just plain stopped. Our ascent up the tree has been blocked, and our questions have not led us to successive limbs to pursue.

In these situations, you may want to *disturb*.

There is a school of thought that says we must disturb the prospect. One of our trainers used to say, "*You gotta make 'em mad!*" And it is frequently easy to get our prospects angry.

Think about it. There is a veritable army of institutions and individuals who are out to take what they have.

There is the IRS, of course, but there is more. There are accountants, fictitious creditors, ex-spouses, plaintiff lawyers, identity thieves, disgruntled employees and customers, and a host of others who stand between a prospect's life's work and his or her family.

Estate taxes have been on and off the table in recent years. For most of us, they are currently off the table, but don't count them out over the long run! Most importantly, remember that estate planning has to do with much more than taxes.

It is a huge mistake for our students to think that just because an estate tax may not currently be likely, the need for estate planning has diminished

At the FSN Summits, we spend as much time as ever on the importance of the many estate planning issues that affect most of our clients. One of the most onerous of these can be probate.

Let's look at probate as an inflection point in building rapport with prospects. Nationally recognized estate attorney Julius Giarmarco calls probate "a voluntary tax you impose on yourself."

What is wrong with probate?

For a start, it often generates completely unnecessary costs. The costs can run anywhere from 6 percent to 10 percent of an estate, and these are dollars the family will never receive.

There are also inherent delays. These delays can range anywhere from six months to two or three years. This is a frustrating time for the family because they don't have complete control over their own assets, and what's more, they must relive the client's death every day.

The family's total affairs will be subject to public record, exposing the family to the claims of fictitious creditors, as well as making private information available to friends, enemies, creditors, employees, and competitors.

And you don't need to die to have a probate disaster. All you need to do is get sick.

Living probate is public in every sense of the word.

It is humiliating because physical, mental, emotional, and monetary facts are exposed and readily available to anyone, from morbid curiosity seekers to gold diggers. *That makes probate a great conversation opener!*

So where do our questions fit into this? Let's look at the FSN process.

Step 1: Ask informational questions to determine exposure to probate.

[*Note:* If you are not familiar with probate exposure, make it a point to learn what does and what does not go through probate.]

> ➤ "How are your assets titled? Are they in your name? Are they jointly titled in your and your wife's name? Or are they in a trust?"
> ➤ "What type of trust do you have?"
> ➤ "Do you remember funding your trust?"

Step 2: If the prospect's answers indicate that there will be a probate problem, you may wish to utilize the following tactic.

An associate of ours has used this tactic frequently with great success, but we have two warnings: *first, he is an expert in probate exposure, and second, this may be too aggressive for your tastes.*

> *We intentionally include a large menu of questions, not all of which are necessary to make the intended point. Still, the language is priceless.*

He prints this out for the prospective client and asks that said prospect call the attorney who drafted the document.

"My financial adviser tells me that an excessive amount of my assets will go through probate, resulting in unnecessary costs, delays, and publicity. Is this true? If so, why haven't you brought it to my attention?

"My financial adviser tells me that I have a testamentary trust, which means that my assets must pass through probate before the trust can become fully operational. Is this true? If so, why haven't you brought it to my attention?"

"My financial adviser tells me that I have an excessive amount of jointly titled property. He called this the 'worst of all worlds' because it misses the bypass trust entirely and will be subject to probate at the second death. Additionally, he says that only half of the value of the property will receive a step up in basis at the first death, resulting in unnecessary capital gains tax should my joint tenant sell the property during his or her lifetime. Is this true? If so, why haven't you brought it to my attention?"

"My financial adviser tells me that I have 'incidents of ownership' in my life insurance. He says that will cause the death benefits to be included in my estate and will be subject to federal estate taxes. Is this true? If so, why haven't you brought this to my attention?"

"My financial adviser tells me that my assets are eligible for discounts through the use of family limited partnerships or family limited liability companies. Is this true? If so, why haven't you brought it to my attention?"

"My financial adviser tells me that I can reduce my estate tax substantially through the use of what he calls 'tax-free transfers.' He says these include statutory GRATs, SCINs, and private annuities. How many of these techniques have you implemented in the past year?

"My financial adviser tells me that these are an integral part of a 'zero estate tax' plan. Is this true? If so, why haven't you brought it to my attention?"

"My financial adviser tells me that a charitable lead annuity trust can be established at my death. He tells me that would enable my family to use a 'supporting organization' and control the donor's committee in order to fund a charitable foundation. He tells me that after a number of years, the trust's balance will be returned to my family free of estate tax, whereas the foundation can remain in force forever. Is this true? If so, why haven't you brought it to my attention?"

This is *very aggressive*, and you may want to tone it down or not use it at all. Of course, it is unlikely anyone would use all of these questions in a single situation.

Our associate has found this tool to be extremely effective and tells us that this has produced more thank-you notes from clients and more referrals than any other single method.

Feel free to use as much or as little as you like, but please be aware that all too often, estate planning documents have been drafted to *intentionally* create probate.

While we believe that most attorneys are professionals of integrity, we are regrettably aware that some law firms do intentionally create probate.

> *When you consider that betrayal by someone you trusted is worse than being cheated by a stranger, you will quickly understand why this was included.*

Questions for the Business Owner

Business owners are faced with more challenges than perhaps any other segment of the population. They raise capital, work around the clock, and can lose everything in a heartbeat. Their income is taxed when they make it, their assets are taxed when they own them, and if their estates are of sufficient size, the IRS may tax them when they die.

We have been lulled into a sense of false security by recent changes to the estate tax rates. We no longer feel that we need to even address the issue.

Nothing could be further from the truth.

Let's do a Harvard case study:

The business owner is Bob Prospect, age fifty-nine.

He is married. His wife, Carol, is age fifty-seven.

They have three children: daughter, Susan, age thirty-six; son Bob Jr., age thirty-four; and son Bill, age thirty-one.

Bob Prospect founded AHM Incorporated in 1983 at age twenty-five. AHM is a plastics injection molding company servicing the automobile industry in Detroit, Michigan.

Bob began on a shoestring. He got a contract with larger plastics injection molding companies to produce parts that exceeded their capacity. Bob borrowed the money to buy his first injection molding machine and worked six days a week to keep his customers happy.

Over time, he added a second machine and hired another employee. Within a few years, he had ten machines, all operated by employees, and he set out to make the company bigger.

By 1995 he grew to the point that AHM became what is called a tier one supplier, and he dealt directly with General Motors.

Bob Jr. joined the company in 2004 and was gifted 1 percent of the stock. Out of convenience, AHM maintained its C corporation status, and the family established a Section 302 redemption agreement. AHM purchased a $7 million life insurance policy such that upon Bob's death, the family would redeem the stock, making Bob Jr. the 100 percent owner and allowing the family to receive the $7 million proceeds from the life insurance.

Bob and Carol's daughter, Susan, is a single mom, and their son Bill is a doctor.

When you call on Bob, he is cordial, but he tells you that all is well. He and his wife own the building and other investment property, as well as a cottage on a lake and a thirty-eight-foot pleasure yacht. He estimates his net worth to be around $10 million and doesn't see any need for your services.

He sends you down the hall to his human resources manager, who asks you to quote on their group health insurance and requests that you get back to them if you can save them over 10 percent of the premium.

You go back to the office, check on group insurance rates, and find that any savings would be negligible. You call the human resources manager and tell him the news. He thanks you for your time and hangs up.

You sigh and realize that tomorrow is another day.

Before you go on, stop and reflect.

What questions could you, and should you, have asked?

How could this have been turned into a successful case?

This is a real case. The names and ages have been changed, but this truly was the situation.

The difference is that when Bob suggested going down the hall to talk to the HR department, the producer asked a series of questions, as follows:

> ➤ "You mentioned that you have a stock redemption agreement. Can you tell me about it?"
> ➤ "Does AHM own the policy?"
> ➤ "Is AHM the beneficiary?"
> ➤ "Are you aware of the tax consequences your family faces?"
> ➤ "Did you know that life insurance owned by a C corporation is a tax-preference item and subject to the alternative minimum tax, roughly 18 percent, which would be about $1.25 million?"

➤ "Did you know that Section 318 prevents this from being a capital transaction?"

➤ "Did you know that the entire $7 million when received by your family will be treated as essentially a dividend and will be fully taxable, at roughly $3.2 million? And don't forget the company will have already paid the alternative minimum tax of $1.25 million, so how will they even pay the full amount to the family?"

➤ "Did you know that Bob Jr. won't get a step-up in basis in this transaction, so when he ultimately sells the company, he will have to pay capital gains tax? At a rate of 25 percent, the first $7 million he receives will be subject to $1.75 million."

➤ "Why don't you call your attorney and ask him if this is true. Oh, be sure to tell him that he can't waive attribution at death because TEFRA specifically excludes the Rickey case."

The producer wrote these points down for the prospect, who called his attorney the next day and asked him if this was true. This was similar to the "My Financial Adviser Tells Me" questions we posed earlier.

The attorney sputtered and asked for time to do some research. Eventually, he called and admitted he was in over his head.

The producer turned this into a win-win situation and included the attorney in the process. He invited him to attend the meetings with another attorney who specialized in this type of tax law.

A proper buy and sell had been established, which reduced the aforementioned potential taxes to zero. New life insurance was purchased because the transfer-for-value rules prevented the son from buying the existing policy from the company. The existing corporate-owned policy was placed into an ILIT (irrevocable life insurance trust) for the main benefit of the daughter, a single mother.

Everybody won.

Let's go further into the AHM case. Let's assume the company is an LLC and that the stock redemption problems do not exist.

What would you do?

Again, before you go on, stop and reflect. What questions could you, and should you, have asked?

How could this have been turned into a successful case?

Analysis

This family has several problems, even with the stock redemption issue not being a factor.

Susan, the daughter, is a single mother and probably could use some help.

Bill, the youngest son, is a doctor and likely is not in need of the same assistance.

Bob Jr. needs to be able to run the company unencumbered by his siblings.

Bob and Carol own their principal residence, a cottage, and a thirty-eight-foot yacht, both of which are eligible for QPRTs (Qualified Personal Residence Trust) or charitable gifts.

Bob and Carol have excessive jointly titled property.

Here are some possible questions:

"Did you know that your jointly titled assets won't get into your trust?"

"Does it concern you that your trust may fail to do what you think it will do?"

"Are you aware, Bob, that should your wife remarry, a second husband could quite possibly inherit everything from your wife, leaving nothing for your children?"

"How does that make you feel knowing you could unintentionally disinherit your own children?"

"Were you aware that if you leave the business equally to your three children, you could harm all of them and possibly sink the company?"

"Is it important to you that AHM survive your death?"

"If Bob Jr. only owns one-third of the company, he can be outvoted by his siblings. Did that ever occur to you?"

"Does it concern you that he could be handcuffed by his siblings?"

"Susan, as a single mother, would likely need income. Where would that come from if she were to receive stock?"

"What are your feelings toward helping her raise her family?"

"Did you know the IRS will give you a tax deduction today for a charitable gift that you do not make until after you and your spouse pass away?"

"Would a current tax deduction be helpful to you? How could you use it?"

Bob and Carol could get a nice current tax deduction

and use a QPRT to pass the house to Susan. A second QPRT could pass the boat to Bill. Yes, if the boat provides cooking and sleeping capabilities, it qualifies for a deduction, but we will not go into that here.

"Currently, your estate is not subject to estate taxes. Do you have any idea what the tax laws will be at the time of your death?"

"How do you feel knowing that everything you have built could be destroyed should Congress change the estate tax rates?"

"Did you know that we can remove your entire estate from federal estate taxation, regardless of the tax rates at your death, while you maintain total control during your lifetime?"

"What would it mean to your family if they knew that they were removed from the entire specter of estate taxes for generations to come?"

This list of questions is by no means complete. You most likely have questions you would ask that may be superior to these.

Please note that they conform to the following pattern— they all follow the Power Combination.

These questions are intended to create a realization. We want the prospect to see things for the first time or to see them differently. Do you remember what we said in the introduction? "I do not think I will tell you anything you don't already know. I do think you will be better off if you knew that you knew it."

That applies to our prospects as well. We want them to raise their awareness levels to new heights and know that there are many tools, devices, and methodologies available that will help them change their lives—if only they knew it.

In conclusion, we hope you have had your own realizations, as follows:

> ➤ Discovery is *not* just "fact finding."
> ➤ It is much more than just finding out about our prospects.
> ➤ It is also about our helping our prospects discover themselves.
> ➤ Working together with us, they have realizations.
> ➤ And they discover deeper understandings about their *values*.
> ➤ That result cannot be engineered. It can only originate from the *perspective* of the prospect.

Rao-ism #31

Intuition will tell the thinking mind where to look next.

PART 3

YOUR WORK, MEMORIALIZED FOR ALL TO SEE!

The Financial Services Network:

Philosophy
Process
Predictions

(8)

THE FSN PHILOSOPHY

Perception is strong, and sight is weak. In strategy it is important to see distant things as if they were close and to take a distant view of close things.

—Miyamoto Mushashi, legendary Japanese swordsman

NOW THAT we have established some ground rules for the FSN Client Acquisition Process, we need to pause for a *values and beliefs review.*

Like our sales process, FSN is values driven. Our commitment to students and members runs deep.

We know we are asking our students and members to take a leap of faith when they agree to transition to our sales process and the software that supports it. As we proceed with the third leg of our guide to contemporary selling, it is important that we all be on the same page. This is because the next step of this guide promises to literally turn some traditional thinking upside down!

Some may find our philosophy and sales process quite palatable because we are only validating many of their current practices and beliefs. After all, we make no claim to ownership of the toolkit, just the process that ties it all together.

Still, *for most, transitioning to the FSN Client Acquisition Process will be a paradigm shift.*

For everyone who moves forward with our process, there will be philosophical agreement as well as some disagreement. As we have emphasized throughout, we are not trying to change any FSP's best practices.

We are, however, proposing a fundamental approach to the Client Acquisition Process, one that requires buying in to our philosophy and core beliefs about the future of the independent FSP in our industry, with things like values-based questions and charging fees.

With this in mind, we put forth the following suppositions, followed by several of our philosophical views on what FSN and our Client Acquisition Process has in store for our students and members:[3]

> ➢ The future of manually delivered financial services belongs to those who can build relationships that are based upon those things that the prospect cannot easily get elsewhere. This will likely require specialization.
> ➢ By layering a specialty over their current practice, FSPs can become focused on those things that make them indispensable to clients.
> ➢ Proper discovery is essential to establishing competency and building trust, allowing prospects to cross over and agree to the payment of a fee before seeing a proposal.
> ➢ To be relevant going forward, FSPs must wean themselves from the product performance and numbers game. Solutions that are strategic and values driven are what facilitate informed decisions on behalf of the

---

[3] Although these beliefs have long been a point of reference for us, Chapter 11 provides a summary of current regulatory direction that appears to make them more mandate than option.

client. *This is the safe harbor provided by the FSN Client Acquisition Process.*

➢ Objectivity is essential when charging a fee, and charging a fee is essential to eliminating the traditional obstacles to a successful client relationship.

➢ Going forward, much of our advice to clients will be subject to third-party evaluations of the customer's best interests and our objectivity. This kind of oversight may dramatically change the landscape of the profession and the accountability of the independent FSP.

If we're good with that, here are our core beliefs about our purpose at FSN:

On Mentors

We think of our mentors as those with whom we have had an impactful and very personal relationship. We believe that these are must-have relationships, but this guide cannot help FSPs with such personal choices.

There is, however, a second kind of mentoring that can be of equal importance, especially in times of change.

During our long careers, we have received important counsel from a different kind of mentor. These mentors were the vanguards of three separate eras in financial product sales. They taught us mostly from afar, but they taught us well.

First were our industry elders, who back in the seventies and eighties existed in abundance. They were mostly known from a distance, as we heard them speak and we read their books. Their advice was the voice of experience.

Wisdom and generosity are the two things that come to mind.

It's important to point out that in those times, just about

anything that worked for them could work for our generation too. (This is another thing that has changed.)

Then, as we have already discussed in detail, things began to change. To a large degree, long-term problems based on fear of loss gave way to product-driven selling. As most of us know, research has since shown us that *fear of loss is a significantly more effective motivator than desire for gain.*

This is especially true in the affluent markets.

This changing situation led to our second source of counsel, who began to appear sometime during the massive changes in the late 1980s. These mentors were all about coping with the future and adapting to change.

Industry events all featured authors of books reminiscent of *Future Shock*, by Alvin Toffler, and *Age Wave*, by Ken Dychwald. Even sophomoric bromides like *Who Moved My Cheese?* were best sellers! Their messages were all about change and what it meant to us. Conditions were changing, and that meant we needed to change our sales practices or become irrelevant.

Those mentors were right. Ironically, huge companies that had been synonymous with innovation, like Kodak and Xerox, resisted change, and today no longer exist.

For many, change is a killer.

Before you think we are stuck too much in the past, keep in mind the good news, which is that while we were losing sight of some of those key traits that built our industry, others on the more progressive front were giving us updated and improved tools. This became the third wave of counsel we benefited from and continue to benefit from today.

These mentors appeared around the new millennium and introduced language that elevated the questioning techniques of yesterday's masters. They were rewriting the basics of selling, with a values-based approach that was more sophisticated and more client inclusive than any of the earlier sales training.

The fact that we spent the last two chapters on discovery says enough about its importance to the FSP Client Acquisition Process. The handful of visionary producers and educators who developed it have been recognized in this guide and by the content of the Discovery Process and the Decision Process software.

We bring this up once more to point out that since values-based discovery was introduced over two decades ago, the situation has changed dramatically.

To overcommunicate again, we say that proper discovery addresses two converging factors that make it more important than ever for the FSP:

> ➤ It is immune to intrusion technology.
> ➤ It is essential for documentation of proper suitability, objectivity, and best interest.

For today's FSP, proper discovery is no longer just a valuable skill. *It is an ethical and regulatory imperative.*

On Staying in the Game

The only thing more dangerous than failure to adapt to change is failure to recognize the boundary between behaviors and values.

Behaviors, practices, and even beliefs can be adapted to accommodate a changing environment, but here's the distinction:

> *Regardless of how much our environment changes and how well we may adapt to it, we must remember that our values can never be compromised to accommodate change.*

125

With many of the traditional means by which we serve our customers under siege, we must establish a game plan for responding. This will likely involve setting some new boundaries. Let's look at an example:

It is our belief that many who represent themselves as comprehensive financial planners, or the equivalent, may be headed for a serious struggle.

No offense to the thousands of financial planners who serve the middle and upper middle markets. How many households in the middle class of the United States would have taken a proactive stance on planning for and ensuring the occurrence of the important financial events of their futures had they not been approached by a planner, adviser, or insurance agent?

The economic impact and social relevance the insurance and financial planning industry has provided to middle-class Americans is incalculable. That said, the reality we are confronted with is this:

Most of Middle America no longer wants to pay a premium for something that has become a commodity.

One reason is because, like it or not, many of the functions in the financial planning process have been surrendered to computer-generated reports. It's no secret that the basics of financial planning for the middle and upper middle market lend themselves to numerically driven templates.

Calculating what is needed to pay off the mortgage and sustain the family in the event of premature death; the cost of a college education and other goals; targeting a retirement date and lifetime income needs; even calculating the present value of an employee's stock options—all these are things that have made financial planners valuable.

Here's the problem:

It just isn't the rocket science it seemed to be in 1990.

Calculators for these and just about every other financial goal are available online, often for free.

Other online tools can mix and match these calculations into a credible financial plan for middle-income Americans, often by using the same tools that the financial planner uses!

In a world where customers pay for advice rather than purchasing a product, financial advisers may find it difficult to justify charging for this level of service.

Our advice to comprehensive planners is this:

Keep doing what got you to where you are but consider layering a specialty on top of your value proposition that is beyond the reach of technology.

Many of our students have already heard a more eloquent version of our advice from the great personal coach and legendary mentor to champions Dan Sullivan. Mr. Sullivan's famous mantra is "Identify your unique ability and focus all of your resources toward perfecting it." Then *"Delegate everything except your genius."* This is regarded as some of the best advice ever given by any coach or mentor.

On Intrusion Technology

Technology being developed by product providers and software entrepreneurs is rolling over journeymen insurance agents and financial planners like a tidal wave.

That genie is out of the bottle, and many FSPs are searching for ways to differentiate themselves. They are well advised to do so.

The unvarnished truth is that the financial institutions that sponsor much of these self-directed offerings have a different horizon than the rest of us. Their goal is to be perpetual and to serve their customers for generations to come. Doing so is their primary responsibility to their bosses, the shareholders. This is their mission. And yes, they too are well advised to do so.

There is no value judgment here, just a situation that is the boss.

Financial institutions are looking toward a time when their relationships with their customers will be seamless and uninterrupted by any human touch not under their control.

Meanwhile, they continue to introduce technology that supports their independent distribution systems, but most of us have noticed this is becoming progressively more intrusive.

Almost all communications provide a default to the institution. The FSP is seen as a placekick holder that can someday easily be removed.

There is a valid argument on behalf of the institutions that much of this is a result of compliance and regulatory issues. All the same, they are tightening their grip on our customers.

The problem is that the institutional food chain starts with the FSP's customer, not the FSP. True to their mission, most have a plan to reinforce that situation. Like it or not, we have a shared customer who, it appears to us, is being poached.

Nearly all fund families, wire houses, and insurance companies have alternative product and service delivery systems that circumvent the FSP. A close look at much of the newest technology usually shows that it is designed to progressively diminish the human component. After all, that is the nature of most technology.

The FSN solution is simple. Like the institutions, our technology is both cutting edge and customer-centric. We have only one customer: the FSP.

For our customer, technology is anything but intrusive. It's indispensable!

On Deciding to Offer a Specialty

When considering offering a specialty, our first piece of advice is to proceed with caution. One more time: don't change anything that is working in your practice, even if it's not what you ultimately want for the future.

When implementing core changes to any business, the new must be introduced gradually and in tandem with that which is being phased out.

How do we know?

Look back at what we've been summarizing about the financial institutions. While many are telling us they've got our backs, few consider us their link to the future. They're doing exactly what they should be doing: adapting!

We suggest the independent FSP do the same.

One answer is to specialize, which for many may mean moving upmarket. We suggest upgrading your clientele through something we call proactive attrition.

Over the course of a designated period (usually annually), the FSP replaces the bottom 20 percent of less profitable relationships with the new 5 percent to 10 percent he or she acquires as a specialist. This will take discipline and a commitment to adapting to create your future.

What does being a specialist really mean?

First, there is more than one definition.

As we've discussed, the FSN approach is for FSPs to specialize in problems that affect their chosen market. In the case of the authors, that chosen market is business owners and self-employed professionals. We may offer clients advice on several problems, but our specialty for our market is the accumulation and distribution of wealth, with the emphasis on safety and taxes.

Those are only two options. The important thing is to layer something over your chosen market that moves your practice to the next level while minimizing any disruption. Part of that next level should include a safe harbor from intrusion technology.

As already discussed, the FSP offering holistic financial planning has a bumpy road ahead. The resolution of many of the problems in the middle market no longer requires the level of manual intervention it once did.

In addition, those who attempt to provide comprehensive services are facing unprecedented exposure to scrutiny, second-guessing, and worse by numerous third parties. In short, being a generalist can be fraught with exposure.

Again, we don't want to discourage anyone who is enjoying success in their chosen market from continuing as they are. We do, however, suggest that they consider redefining their value proposition to adapt to the emerging situation.

Before any readers feel intimidated by the notion of specializing in the problems of the affluent business owner, or any other market, remember this:

> *Your specialty is first with the problem. Next you consider select solutions.*

Here's the good news: Our advice above is validated by most of our members. They want no part in trying to be all things to clients, especially at the upper levels of income or wealth. It's way too ambitious an undertaking.

Even the high-end financial planners who penetrate this market are seeing their landscape change. Few are still both asset gatherers and money managers. Almost none are still stock pickers or promoters of private placements or even private equity.

Most are shedding items from their own menus, so we need not worry about them claiming enough expertise in our specialty to interfere. Our approach is narrow but deep.

We help a specific type of prospect solve specific problems in which we specialize.

The problems of the upper market may appear somewhat different from those of the middle and upper middle market of many of our readers, but they are not. We would argue that, underneath, there is less difference than one might imagine.

Yes, the problems can be complex and esoteric. Yet often they revolve around two basic issues: *minimizing taxes and maximizing spendable income.*

We feel that any resourceful and coachable FSP who has clients or who can get in front of prospects who have these two concerns is a candidate for this specialty. It is important to note that they need not be in the high-income market.

For example, the FSP who is centered in the middle market can layer a specialty over her general planning practice, such as retirement and distribution planning. This strategy would typically place emphasis on the IRA market, which contains enormous wealth and opportunity for creative planning. With ten thousand baby boomers retiring every day, we believe retirement distribution is one of the biggest opportunities in the history of our industry!

The good news is that there is a learning and training platform for this market that is the gold standard. The Ed Slott organization has long been regarded as the final authority on IRAs, retirement planning, and retirement distribution. We highly recommend that those interested in this market take a close look at this organization. If the reader needs any convincing, Rao Garuda has been a loyal member of the Ed Slott

Group since its inception. For more information, go to their website: IRAhelp.com. By the way, we have no dog in this hunt, other than our positive personal experience.

Regardless of the market, an FSP may select these same two areas: minimize taxes and maximize spendable income. Our guess is that these same concerns are present to some extent in most markets an FSP might consider.

It is the solutions to those problems that will be different.

For example, in the federal employee market there are sound strategies that differ from those of the teacher's market. Even in these markets, where incomes are somewhat moderate, we are convinced that *the future of manually delivered financial advice belongs to the specialist.*

Sound familiar? In Chapter 2, we told you to remember that the stars of the golden age of financial product selling were not financial planners. They solved problems one need at a time.

The indispensable FSP of today should take a similar approach. Like others in the field, they give financial advice, but what the client is paying a premium for is specialized advice that is above and beyond the norm.

Do it right. Do it with competence. Do it with passion. Your reputation will follow with *attraction power* that brings clients to you. It's not that complicated.

On Selecting a Platform

Your platform may be a broker-dealer, IMO, wire house, insurance company, bank, CPA, or law firm. We're not necessarily urging readers to change platforms, but we do think it is something that should be periodically reviewed by the forward-thinking FSP.

This is especially true for those who are independent and

considering the inclusion of a specialization in their value proposition.

There are both strategic and tactical choices that we believe the alert FSP must consider, relative to the operating platform they chose. We don't have a crystal ball, so we submit these actions only as a suggested way of approaching the subject of platform requirements for your future.

> ➤ Along with continuing to do what you do well, identify your unique ability. Then select a specialty that leverages your unique ability. *Note:* This may involve studying the work of Dan Sullivan and, of course, coaching from FSN.
> ➤ Focus your practice on a market that complements your unique ability and that can benefit from your specialty. *Note:* This is somewhat contradictory to most thinking in that we suggest beginning with your unique ability, then picking a specialty, and finally selecting the market(s) that fit(s) that specialty.
> ➤ Review the level of support, compatibility, and commitment that your current platform, as well as other offerings, exhibits toward the foregoing objectives.
> ➤ Based upon what you believe about the future of our industry, give serious thought as to how you can position yourself and your practice strategy on the platform that best serves your chosen market and business model.

Here's our question:

Given the trends with intrusion technology, why would an FSP make a product provider, institutional platform, or broker dealer the central resource for his business if he is not the central resource for their business?

In keeping with our commitment to objectivity when advising our students, we acknowledge that there are other organizations that share our values. Just as they do when evaluating choices for clients, it is important to us that our readers and students examine their options when deciding on a strategy for their future.

A sponsoring platform that has made a strategic commitment to the independent FSP is a likely fit. When we say commitment, we're not talking about the independent FSP being on their short list. We're talking "all in." As an enterprise, they succeed or fail at your side.

We know of only a few platforms that fit this definition. Interestingly, each is arguably the strongest performer in its industry space. (Have we mentioned the value of being a specialist?)

The values of these leading platforms are well known throughout our industry.

The FSP is their one and only customer.

For their strategies to continue working, they must have technology at their FSPs' fingertips—technology *designed specifically for them* that not only can compete favorably with intrusion technology but also can best it in many areas.

On Eliminating Age-Old Obstacles

Sacking the quarterback

Solving the CPA dilemma

Shelving the second opinion

The benefits of specialization extend beyond the good things it brings to clients. Specialization can also make us more focused, which helps to address some of the chronic obstacles we often encounter in the Client Acquisition Process.

We have another belief that is contrary to some current thinking but that may bode well for a strategy focused on specialization:

> *Don't fall for the approach of packaging yourself as a financial "quarterback" who coordinates strategies with the prospect's other advisers.*

The supposed idea is for the quarterback (FSP) to connect the dots between the prospect's various plans, products, programs and assets, then blending his proposal into the mix. Then, as the quarterback and to bring some symmetry to it all, he invites the client's other advisers into the process. The idea being that a proactive offence beats a reluctant defense.

We don't believe in the quarterback approach to teamwork. For starters, it's a very risky business when we try to interpret and review the work of other professionals, especially if we weren't present when the decisions were made. Also, with the QB position comes liability. Who do the people in the stands usually blame when their team loses a game?

Instead, do what you do well and show the prospect how you can bring him value that he cannot easily get elsewhere. Forget the QB analogy. It doesn't work!

How do we know?

First, if you are a specialist, there is little chance that any of your prospect's advisers will understand your recommendations well enough to give them a pass, let alone get behind them—and certainly not well enough to bless them. And no matter how you frame it, those advisers will take your prospect's invitation as a request for their blessing.

Here's our question:

How many FSPs do you know who have built a successful model working with their prospects' other financial advisers as a chosen strategy?

Proponents of this approach paint a picture of the financial team sitting around the client's conference table singing "Kumbaya."

We don't think so! This approach is a defensive hedge at best, and as such it is a risky offer to put forth to prospects.

Here's another departure from the traditional approach:

In most cases, we prefer being isolationists when it comes to other plans or financial strategies the prospect may have. We want to avoid being put in the position of being deemed an "expert" just because we volunteered an opinion on things we may not be qualified to pass judgment on. We don't like that exposure.

The only reason we look at a prospect's other plans has to do with the *cash flow modeling we do to show the impact of our recommendations on the prospect's overall situation. Not to compete or compare, but simply to show the impact on the prospect's cash flow that our recommendations may have.*

This brings us to an important issue about the most common obstacle with larger cases, especially those involving tax strategies: *the CPA.*

We believe that as the designated specialist, we can often fend off any inclination by the prospect to seek a second opinion from her CPA or anyone else.

Once the prospect has *crossed over and paid a fee*, the idea of having the CPA or other advisers brought in to review your work often fades.

How do we know?

The client has skin in the game!

Transitioning to fees can solve a lot of problems for the adviser of the future.

What this means to you is that should the client entertain

the idea of getting a second opinion from his CPA, you have a new and powerful response:

> *"Would your CPA be okay with me signing off on your tax returns? That's what you pay her for. You've already paid me for the same level of expert counsel"*

Thus, our short answer for most FSPs: If this is a door you can close and keep closed, keep the CPA out of the process.

This has nothing to do with sales practices, compliant behavior, or ethics. It is simply common sense. If you are a specialist, you can rest assured that in almost every case, the CPA, or any other service provider bought in by your prospect, will be clueless as to your proposals. If they know anything at all, it usually will be just enough to be dangerous. That may be the last honest answer they give you!

What possible upside could there be for them to vote for a concept a stranger asks their client to put money into? They would be foolish to put their reputation with their client on the line for you! Not to mention the downside if it doesn't work out as planned. Who can blame them for not buying in?

Our advice is to leave any teamwork with your prospect's other advisers to the larger high-end planning firms and family offices. They have real teams of their own who *all wear the same jersey*!

That said, if you can build a qualified team *within your specialty*, that's an entirely different matter. It is also a primary purpose of FSN.

To be perfectly clear, we are indeed encouraging the FSP to build a team of their own specialists. Just be sure the team members are within *the silo of your specialty*. Stick to your comfort corridor: minimizing taxes and maximizing spendable income (or whatever specialty you chose). FSN is likely to have outstanding candidates for building that team. Professionals within your specialty that all wear the same jersey!

Like with most of our advice, we understand that there will be exceptions to our general rules. *Working around the CPA is probably the one for which we are most accustomed to agreeing to exceptions.*

Sometimes, despite our preferences, the prospect is going to insist on a second pair of eyes that she trusts.

When the prospect has a CPA that she is going to involve in the case you are working on, we have one crucial piece of advice:

> *Bring the CPA in at the very beginning or walk away. No exceptions.*

In our experience, the CPA is usually brought in by the prospect sometime after the adviser's initial presentation.

The FSP, thinking that a CPA is a numbers guy, then shows him the solution she is proposing and tries to explain it by walking him through the numbers.

Here's our question:

> *If leading with the solution doesn't work with the prospect, why would you think it would work with the CPA? The CPA thinks you're just trying to sell his client something, and you validate his concern by doing a sales presentation!*

The CPA needs to see how you came to the recommendations being considered right from the very beginning. He must understand the problem that has been uncovered, what solutions are being considered, and why.

Yes, CPAs are numbers people, but the typical proposal

focuses on the end result. That means nothing to a CPA, unless you can show them where every number came from.

That's what they do. It's called auditing!

Guess what? If you earn the respect and trust of the CPAs, just as you did with the prospect, they may even *cross over* and get on board. In some cases, they may even become rainmakers for you!

If our advice on CPAs sounds ambiguous, that's because it is a very lopsided opportunity. Few CPAs feel they can align themselves with FSPs because they have nothing in common with us. They make their living by documenting things that have already happened, while we make our living by planning for things that have yet to happen.

Occasionally, you will come across one of those rare CPAs with a windshield bigger than their rearview mirror. These are CPAs we can work with because of the one thing we do have in common: the best interests of our mutual client, even if it means going out of the CPA's comfort zone to learn something new.

For these CPAs, our different perspectives complement one another and pose a unique opportunity. The type of CPA who welcomes this type of relationship is rare, so if you can build a solid relationship with even one of them, you are one up on 90 percent of your competition.

Whether you have a CPA who has crossed over or you have one you are in the process of building a relationship with, you may want to bring him or her to an FSN event. There your CPA colleague will meet not only other CPAs but also lawyers, investment bankers, money managers, and other financial professionals.

We specifically do not attempt to recruit CPAs. That's your job. As we mentioned earlier, the idea of mass recruiting CPAs, or matching them with advisers in a classroom setting, just doesn't work. CPAs and other potential rainmakers don't "get sold" on or "recruited to" anything. When they attend an event, they don't want to feel there is a target on their back.

At FSN events, we inform and educate CPAs on financial strategies and provide a platform to network with like-thinking financial professionals. They will interact with other quality FSPs and hear from an eclectic and highly credentialed faculty.

Our approach works because the FSP already has enough of a relationship to get the CPA, lawyer, or other professional to attend our event. The value we bring is genuine because the purpose of the meeting is *not* to sell them on working with the FSP. Instead they are there to learn things that are of value to them.

We acquaint them with a means of easing themselves into the proactive world of building *their* business by bringing new value to *their* clients and additional billable hours to *their* firm. That's what attracts them to working with us.

The only way CPAs move forward on a proactive partnership with an FSP is by taking incremental steps. The only leap they are going to take is the leap of faith that the FSP is the real deal—competent and trustworthy.

Consider this approach and pull back on the hard sell. Know that you are looking for genuine exceptions. Those few who are real candidates for an alliance will come to you for those things they cannot easily get elsewhere.

On the FSN Mission

The Financial Services Network was created to educate, train, and mentor FSPs from all segments of the financial services industry, with emphasis on innovation. Our purpose is to teach FSPs how to live up to their chief responsibility: *helping clients make informed decisions about their financial future.*

We provide a forum for advisers that combines the voice

of experience and cutting-edge technology with the chemistry that occurs when an eclectic group of established professionals gather.

Our faculty consists of the industry's leading financial professionals, marketers, and mentors, along with creators of the most innovative strategies.

Our training and education are centered on the FSN Client Acquisition Process and the proprietary software that supports it, which provides our members a clear path to achieving indispensability. A path that can lead some of our students to advanced markets and specialization. For others, it will simply codify their position in their existing market. For all, it will provide the key to avoiding irrelevance by using tools and ideas to make the adviser indispensable to clients—a process that can establish objectivity and suitability in the process the FSP uses to procure clients.

Our focus begins and ends with our students and members. Our proprietary technology is designed to deliver the client information to the FSP's doorstep and to give the FSPs the key to the vault which they and their clients control.

We believe in the power of the human touch in the rendering of financial advice, and we have tailored everything we do to strengthen that touch.

Rao-ism #24

At first something may seem impossible. Then it becomes improbable. With enough conviction and support, it becomes inevitable.

9

The Decision Process

When possible, make decisions now, even if the action is in the future. A reviewed decision is usually better than one made at the last minute.

—William B. Given

AMONG THE many aspects of the sales process that have been surrendered to the Trojan horse we call intrusion technology; case design is our greatest concern.

Sales technology has done a superb job of not only providing boilerplate solutions but also, with the guidance and oversight of the FSP, doing complete and sophisticated plans that include levels of detail, footnotes, and drill-down that most of us could not easily get elsewhere.

Historically, this successful relationship was made possible by support from various financial institutions and wholesaling firms that routinely provided arm's-length internal resources to answer any question the FSP, the client, or even their CPA might have.

We usually would incorporate this input, along with that of the client, as interpreted by the FSP, into a plan that used technology to help refine, perfect, and package it, but not to make value judgments in the design or to implement.

All of this is progress for our clients that we welcome.

Currently, however, technology is being introduced to perform the act of case analysis (reviewing the problem or needs) and replacing the human and advanced market resources that were housed by the wholesaling and product manufacturers to support the adviser with the design and implementation.

Positions like advanced underwriting and advanced case design, which used to be housed in large departments in the wire houses and insurance carriers, are no more. If they do still exist, it's more for defensive reasons. Their role seems to have gone from how to get a case done as their priority to how to avoid risk as their priority. We're not talking about the client's risk or your risk either!

Even the people who underwrite the business, be it life insurance or financial underwriting, are being replaced by software programs. For us, underwriting is as much an art as it is a science. Sadly, for those who control these functions, that widely held notion is being ignored.

In short, the camel called artificial intelligence has gotten its nose under the tent. By the way, who wants expert advice that is rendered by resources that are "artificial"? *Talk about a contradiction in terms!*

Who's next? Not the qualified FSPs who embrace the FSN Client Acquisition Process. What we have in store for you in the point-of-sale arena will be a game changer. *Guaranteed!*

You've probably figured out by now that we're not talking about selling an insurance policy, investment, or other financial product here. This is not to say that this may not be one of the results, because we really don't know what we are going to recommend without proper discovery and case design.

Most of the time, however, we are referring to a strategy

that offers innovative concepts or similar specialized benefits in addition to product performance. That often means we're working in the upper-income and advanced markets. In the end, no matter who the prospect is, someone must decide. That's where the Decision Process software comes in.

We don't deny that plan implementation is a euphemism for closing the sale.

All the same, we feel that, in our market, telling an FSP she is a "great closer" is an insult.

Why do we say this?

Let's pause before going into the implementation phase to look at some important scientific work that concludes with this:

> *Closing is* not *a significant part of the FSN Client Acquisition Process, nor should it be a part of any sophisticated sales process. Instead, we should provide resources and information to help the prospect make an informed decision.*

In 1989, exactly thirty years after *The Five Great Rules of Selling* was published, the second great book of our age on selling was introduced in London, England. *Spin Selling* was authored by marketing research guru Neil Rackham, PhD.

In our opinion, it became the gold standard among all books for sales training written from that point to the present, including those books written by us during that period.

Perhaps it is no coincidence that after yet another thirty years—in 2019—our definitive guide to the future of selling financial services has finally been published. One can only hope!

In his classic book *Spin Selling*, Dr. Rackham delivers some groundbreaking research. Over a period of several years, he studied over thirty-five thousand individual sales calls! He learned a lot, so we strongly recommend the book to our readers who haven't yet read it. We first learned of and tried some of the discovery ideas outlined in *From Irrelevant to Indispensable* after reading this great book.

For us, one of Dr. Rackham's most interesting findings is regarding the size and complexity of a sale. The greater the price of the purchase and the more complicated it is, the more the decision to buy or not to buy becomes obscured, until, toward the end of the process, it becomes axiomatic.

Years ago, when the rest of us were having a debate about who owns the customer, it was Dr. Rackham who pointed out, *"The customer owns the customer!"*

This tracks well with what we have been discussing so far. For many readers, the book's biggest revelation is this:

> *It is not how we sell that we need to learn more about. It is how our customer makes a buying decision. That decision is based upon information and choices that, if not addressed by the salesperson, are likely to be sought and acted upon elsewhere by the prospect.*

Dr. Rackham begins his study of the way customers buy with the most impulsive and inexpensive purchases. Things like a key chain one may spot at an airport newsstand. Not a lot of thought goes into adding a key chain to the purchase of a newspaper, a magazine, and a bag of peanuts.

We all know that as we move up the socioeconomic spectrum, the process of buying becomes more and more complicated.

What the research in *Spin Selling* shows is that Percy H. Whiting was right: the decision by a prospect to move forward involves a series of smaller decisions, just as his book told us thirty years earlier.

The big difference is that today those steps are achieved *not by the persuasive skills of the sales representative, but by a series of judgments from the buyer, based upon the information provided by the sales representative.*

Dr. Rackham goes all the way up the buying chain to the example of a mainframe computer, which in 1989 was about as big a purchase a company could consider. We might add that anyone involved in that process back then (as one of your authors was) knows that the projected promises of a mainframe computer salesperson far exceeded anything we would have dared to promise with a financial strategy proposal!

The bottom line is that by the time the request to buy / go forward with major purchases, be it a mainframe computer or a sophisticated investment or tax strategy, *the decision has already been made.*

If the salesperson has done his or her job, there's little in the way of closing to be done. In truth, at this point the sale is the FSP's to lose.

Dr. Rackham's work further suggests that in most situations, when we do not gain agreement to move forward, it is usually for one of three reasons:

> ➤ The FSP failed to do proper *discovery.*
> ➤ The FSP failed to build enough *trust.*
> ➤ The prospect did not fully *understand* the proposal.

We covered discovery in Chapters 6 and 7, but we suspect most FSPs will need a lot more work to become "unconsciously competent" at it.

We addressed trust in our discussion on relationship building in Chapter 4 and again in our discussion of the crossover. By this point, prospects should feel that you are providing something they cannot easily get elsewhere.

That leaves only the understanding of our proposal.

Here's where we go off the rail again, so hold on to your hat!

The Decision Process software is just that. It offers choices that allow the FSP and the prospect to consider alternative solutions to the stated problem—choices for the prospect to consider with the adviser's guidance.

How can offering more choices solve the problem with a prospect who may not understand a single proposal? That's a subject for a larger discussion/debate than we can address in this guide. For now, just know that we are right about it.

The short answer is that the FSN Client Acquisition Process is founded on building trust through competence during our discovery process. Then, when we show the prospect that several options were considered, we establish our objectivity. This is another crossover point.

With our objectivity documented by the Decision Process, the prospect becomes comfortable that we are representing their best interests.

Now, it's up to the FSP to make sure the prospect understands their options. Sometimes, just a brief verbal overview of the alternatives considered is enough. Other situations may require a spreadsheet summary reviewing the choices. Still other situations may require us to use the Decision Process software in a point-of-sale review of the strategies considered, even doing what-if scenarios. Finally, it may involve passing muster with CPAs, attorneys, and our competitors.

The FSP must read the prospect's level of need for making an informed decision. (This is one more nuance beyond the reach of technology!)

We know only too well that there are many examples of adviser practices that are not compatible with this kind of approach.

How do we know?

As previously stated, too many of today's FSPs are still engaged in the antiquated practice of being a solution in search of a problem. The starkest example of this is the disingenuous sales practices used by some life insurance companies that predominately market whole life.

The FSP is trained in a sort of shell game. Whatever direction the discovery process takes, the prospect is guided to the same solution: a customized version of a single product. We are saddened by these tactics, because whole life is arguably the most venerable product in all of financial services.

> *Whole life is always a solid consideration without loading the dice in its favor.*

Although most FSPs do not play the shell game, many tend to stay in their comfort zone and offer prospects customized versions of a single solution. Ironically, it will be technology, and specifically the Decision Process, that will help FSPs break this dangerous cycle.

Our licensed users need never again approach prospects in the hope that the latter will buy into a single solution or product.

By now, it should be clear that in the world we see ahead, the FSN approach of offering credible choices is gaining momentum, with or without our help!

> *Much of that momentum will not be voluntary. Recent trends on the regulatory front are signaling that FSPs will be expected to consider and offer prospects objective choices in proposing solutions to their needs based on their best interests.*

We believe this is a curve that we can help our students get ahead of. Having software and training to render advice may prove to be a huge advantage to early adapters. Of course, the software must be both objective and pass the "best interests" test on behalf of clients. Compliance in these matters is not our purview, but everything we teach is driven by our best practices.

The problem with the technical tools in wide use today is that most exist in a vacuum. Although many can illustrate concepts very effectively, none we know of show the overall impact of the decision on the client's situation.

The Decision Process software provides something that is unprecedented. We show the effect of a given strategy on the prospect's overall financial status. We call this the "ripple effect."

Why is this necessary? Because of magnitude.

Historically, when FSPs helped clients with typical financial choices, the only consideration was the potential result of a single decision to buy an insurance policy or invest in a mutual fund—a single-needs sale.

The strategies proposed by today's specialist serving the upper-income markets have far-reaching consequences. They are not just one of several accumulation strategies that either hit or miss the mark. They are far-reaching and innovative approaches that must be executed with precision and expertise.

All the more reason for specialization.

We are not in the business of proposing isolated concepts that deliver projections on a piece of paper that may later be construed as promises. Actually, in the FSN market, we are often taking on much more. We are diverting considerable assets/income/revenue of the prospect, or their business, into concepts that are often new to them.

Remember—among the affluent and high net worth, the most ubiquitous concern is fear of losing money. Ironically, when we work with these prospects, the relative stakes are often much higher than they are for a middle-income client.

How do we know?

Discontinuing an IRA, discontinuing a mutual fund investment, or even lapsing a life insurance policy doesn't usually carry potentially catastrophic consequences, unless something catastrophic outside the client's control happens in the short term. That's because unless they're seniors, they have time to recover.

Our prospects are usually a decade or older than those in the middle market, and they usually won't have enough time to recover. Also, the strategies they choose often involve the core assets of their business.

Having a tax-advantaged strategy that uses key business assets, or all a successful doctor's surplus income, blow up is catastrophic. If that strategy affects the client's life's work, there is blame to be assigned.

With relevancy comes accountability!

Our prospects not only don't need to take unnecessary risks; they are also notably risk averse. After all, they are taking enough risks with their business or profession without our help! That's why we are so thorough in our discovery and so conservative in our proposals.

The Decision Process is a versatile and sophisticated calculator that is 100 percent under the control of the FSP.

The FSN Decision Process software is a Tool for Information, Not Persuasion

Here's the biggest of our non sequiturs that makes the FSN Client Acquisition Process a game changer: A primary purpose of the FSN Decision Process software is to create a departure from the thing on which all competing software is focused—*columns of numbers based upon multiple assumptions that are accumulated, year by year, leading to a targeted age with an impressive numerical result.*

> *Instead, our focus is on a sound strategy that maximizes the likelihood of a favorable outcome extending beyond ultimate numbers.*

> *It's that simple and that straightforward.*

Thus, several strategies may need to be considered for a desired outcome—an outcome that is chosen because of its structure, its direction, and the comfort level of the prospect. Above all, it is chosen based on the client's values, not driven by numbers that are largely unknowable.

Once again, enthusiasm about projected financial performance should not be the primary reason for moving forward with a strategy. On the contrary, the strategy should stand up to reasonable alternatives under uniformly applied stress testing. That's what our prospects really care about: the risks, not the return!

Our concept presentations often consider illustrations from available software used by the rest of the industry. Then, we usually discount it by an amount that is a function of our caution and prudence. This is the way FSPs of the future should approach their best practices mandate.

How do we know?

As far as we're concerned, the calculators used to project the performance of highly sophisticated strategies and concepts are called "software" for a reason: because their answers are given in soft numbers!

In many cases, the numbers are soft to the point of being mercurial. The spreadsheets and diagrams used to persuade prospects chart performance on a year-to-year basis as if the numbers were real. In truth, not a single number is likely to be precise in the end.

Think about how that indisputable fact can impact the cumulative illustration of a product or concept over a lifetime. Not just any lifetime, but that of your client!

This line of thinking about how to stage recommendations marks a seminal difference between this method and the prevailing practices of most FSPs.

We start by doing the same thing every other financial strategy or proposal does: We review illustrations and numbers that are educated guesses. We run spreadsheets and study product brochures and available information.

The difference is, rather than mitigating the uncertainty of an outcome with columns of numbers and seemingly authoritative decimal points, we round down to the nearest thousand, or more if we deem appropriate. Our objective is to eliminate any notion of precision, certainty, or bias.

This practice does not mean our proposals aren't generally accurate. On the contrary, our conservative process strengthens our credibility.

If the prospect likes our idea and the details about how it might work for him, we charge a fee for a feasibility study that will tailor a recommendation specifically for him.

To be clear: typical prospects in our market understand money and numbers. Either they, or their CPAs, will most certainly want to see the specifics before they move forward.

But the prospect won't move forward, and the CPA won't care about the numbers, until they both understand *why* the proposal is being considered. If they are sold on the problem, the numbers only need to make sense. Then we can show a conservative scenario that does its job, even if things don't work out as well as we hope they will.

How do we explain this unconventional approach to the prospect?

> *We start with a proposal that is customized to the prospect's appearance. Then, if she wants to take the next step, she pays a fee so we can tailor the strategy to her specific dimensions.*

Depending on the complexity of the case and the FSP's style, at the next meeting, we either deliver a specific proposal or, if we have done underwriting and secured an offer, present the actual product we are using to fund the strategy. This is up to the customs of the FSP.

At this time, we may review the Decision Process and remind the prospect why she chose the strategy we are now about to implement.

These are, of course, only highlights of the Client Acquisition Process.

The FSN software is strategy, solution, and company agnostic. As such, it plays a key role between the FSPs and their prospects and clients.

In some situations, the prospect may only see the recommendation favored by the FSP. Usually because that's what the prospect has requested.

In other cases, the client will be engaged in the decision process with a review of the alternatives that are being considered.

The key is that any recommendations arrived at are only proposed after considering a well-documented process—a process that includes the FSP's personal review of each choice being considered.

The paradigm shift that we hope will be refreshing to most

FSPs is that the FSN software considers each choice *without prejudice.*

The Decision Process is as open-ended as we can make it. What we mean by that is, for the market an FSP is focused on, the discovery process is not biased toward a specific recommendation. Rather, it is intended to help the client consider different concepts or strategies on which the FSP has done his or her due diligence.

If you are versed in enough solid alternatives for the problems in which you specialize, you will be a refreshing alternative to other advisers, who routinely approach your prospects with solutions that may or may not fit the problem.

> *The way the FSN Decision Process software works is truly unique to our business.*

For example, it addresses two "elephants in the room" head-on. Along with the strategies being considered, it includes these two options:

> ➢ doing something else
> ➢ doing nothing at all

It's surprising to us how often these options have the opposite effect one might expect and shine a light on our recommendations. Let's look at one example:

A typical prospect who fits our market profile usually has income beyond his lifestyle needs. He often is interested in putting aside money for the future, preferably in something tax-advantaged. If self-employed, he might consider a qualified plan.

So, a defined benefit pension plan would be one of the options we might include in the Decision Process.

What's different is that we will also offer other alternatives that may trade off benefits for flexibility or risk tolerance for returns.

The reason this comprehensive approach works is that the software allows the adviser, and the prospect if the former chooses to engage the latter, to stress-test solutions.

We pit one solution against another and even allow blended solutions.

One example of such a comparison we have run many times might surprise our readers. It demonstrates that in certain situations, a good IUL (Indexed Universal Life) policy, or a good whole life policy, stands up very favorably against a defined benefit pension plan.

This is partially because there are differences that the Decision Process allows the client to weigh based upon his or her insurability, age, and risk tolerance, along with other considerations.

Most importantly, there must be clarity on all the considerations between a qualified plan and a life insurance policy. This typically involves the inclusion of an ERISA-qualified third party, especially if any specific comparisons are made.

> *The FSN software will create an objective apple-to-apple comparison between two or more strategies that share a common performance objective.*

The prospect can provide variable input with things such as retirement age, and we push a button that will allow all the changes to ripple through the side-by-side comparisons.

This we can promise you:

> *The Decision Process is a tool the prospects cannot access elsewhere. They can only access it through one of our licensed advisers.*

That makes it a relationship builder.

How you use the FSN software is your decision.

As with all our teachings, we show great respect for the style and practices that have been developed by FSPs over their selling/advisory careers.

There will be different applications for the Decision Process software, depending upon the personalities of the various prospects and comfort and style of the FSP.

Some will love the idea of engaging the right kind of prospect at the point of sale in actual what-if demonstrations that allow prospects to see the immediate effect of differing assumptions, not only between strategies, but also on the rest of their cash flow.

Others will prefer to use our software behind closed doors, as part of their case work and design. In such cases, we suggest they still provide the other reports at point of sale as backup for how the FSP arrived at the solution being recommend.

Still others may delegate the testing of strategies against one another to their staff. (We recommend FSN software training to all users' staff members.)

Note: It must be remembered that in our business, we can delegate work but not responsibility. Going forward, that statement will be truer than it ever was.

Those who are members of FSN will have access to our internal case work specialists for the Decision Process. Our support staff are not only experts on the Decision Process but also are available for individual training of the FSPs and their staff.

The important thing is for the FSPs to be satisfied that they are living up to their obligation of helping prospects make informed decisions. FSPs and prospects alike now can look at their options in an entirely different light—*a light that is illuminated according to the prospect's values but influenced by the FSP's narrative and expert opinion.*

Perhaps most importantly, for any onlookers, this approach to case work will memorialize the fact that objective and suitable alternatives were considered before a recommendation was acted upon.

A major departure from the norm for us is that we suggest illustrations of concepts and strategies should first be shown for informational purposes only.

Although client specific, our proposals focus on the appropriateness and suitability of the strategy rather than on the performance of the numbers. Before we discuss things like internal rates of return, prospects must first buy in to how the concept being suggested works.

The rest is just promises and guesses on a piece of paper.

We believe this is the right way to influence prospects in choosing you as their FSP.

How one strategy performs under one set of variables has nothing to do with how it performs under another. This is especially true if one of the considered strategies involves life insurance.

We know that some strategies work some of the time for some of our clients, but no strategy works all of the time for all of our clients. Each case is different. Given that fact, we are very troubled by advisers who promote products and strategies that are fundamentally the same from one case to another.

By now the reader knows, *this is a very big issue with FSN.*

Our software will run strategies and contrast them until we obtain information that shows not which is best, but under which circumstances one performs differently than others, and when it does not.

As our licensed users soon learn, proposals have crossover points too!

Only after the qualification process do we deliver a finished product to prospects. It will be both accurate in its purpose and precise in its numbers. Prospects don't need to see how the watch was built, but they do need to know how illustrated results were arrived at. If there's a CPA involved, we can show her how the watch is built, but she will also want to see and understand the problem it addresses.

The most important thing we work toward is that the client's decision be made for the right reasons, including if he chooses to do something else or nothing at all. That means his decision is values and process based, not numbers based—a process that defers to the client, so he can make an informed decision based upon what's important to him!

In fact, it is our view that if the decision is based primarily on the numbers, something wasn't done correctly in the process.

Here's the FSN value we hope you've been waiting for:

The decision by a prospect to implement a plan we recommend should always be driven by three things: personal values, personal situation, and the soundness of the strategy. The numbers are there to provide comfort in the choice, not to make it!

Through discovery we evoke emotions that are deliberately personal and specific. We then earn our fee by delivering fundamentally sound and suitable recommendations with objectivity.

As we learned in our discussion of *Spin Selling*, if there is a sale to be made, it probably occurred in the discovery process, when the prospect crossed over and decided you are competent and trustworthy. Now you want them to make a logical and informed decision. That's what leads to long-term valued client relationships. It also generates more referrals!

> *What matters is that the process is compliant and effective, which reinforces the issue of your*

competence and objectivity. That is what leads to indispensability.

We approach the issue of oversight authorities and market conduct supervision in the same fashion. Integrity, honesty, due diligence, and the golden rule are our guides. We go no deeper than that. The things we believe in never change!

To help our kind of prospect make an informed decision, we also satisfy their need to know something the investment banking world calls "the flow of the deal."

In investment banking, most of prospects know that the numbers on a term sheet are dependent upon the performance of the strategy, not the computer that spits them out. We should approach our prospects with the same respect.

The Decision Process is designed to show accepted, proven solutions. In the process, it shows how a given transaction flows. This is especially valuable to business owners, who are used to considering cash flow in making financial decisions. Those attending our events will learn about the importance we place on cash flow modeling.

For purposes of our training programs, we use mostly fixed investment, insurance, and annuity-based strategies, the specific design and approval of which will be overseen by the appropriate parties the FSP works with.

In the real world, most compliant mainstream financial products, fixed or variable, can be used to implement one of our strategies. We understand the concept of specialization better than most.

Our world is that of the Client Acquisition Process and sound strategies, not the vehicles that fuel them.

The nature of the solutions the FSP prefers, or feels qualified to offer, is up to the individual FSP and the rules governing his or her operating platform.

Like our presentations themselves, our teachings are often generic and have broad application. Our core business is the discovery of problems and the research of solutions that, based upon the prospect's values, may work.

> *Now we are going to begin the process of proposing a draconian change in the way many of the best FSPs will represent themselves to the public in the future.*

Buckets Not Only Solve Problems but Also Contain Your Compensation

For several years there has been a growing movement among FSPs who are focused on the upper market to become RIAs (registered investment advisors) and IRAs (independent registered advisors, under whom RIAs usually operate).

One reason is to narrow the range of their advice and specialize their offerings to clients. To do so, most have deregistered and no longer do investments or receive any commissions or investment management fees. Many have found the high ground, and most are doing very well there.

As our earlier chapters pointed out, many of the early financial planners came from the single-needs background of the life insurance business. They often referred to themselves as "recovering life insurance agents."

Now, for those who can adapt, the next confession may be admitting to being a recovering comprehensive financial planner.

What does this mean for you?

Here, we again defer to the teachings of Dan Sullivan, who clearly owns the answer for most of us by his classic credo:

Identify your unique ability and focus all of your resources on becoming the best at it.

Arguably the greatest personal coach ever is mandating that you be a specialist!

To overcommunicate once more: your specialty is with the problem. For every problem or need, there is usually more than one solution or strategy to be considered.

For each solution the FSP either is the implementation expert or has the appropriate access to the right expert. We suggest the reader build his or her specialization around this simple approach: keep it narrow but deep.

At any given time, there are usually no more than five or six strategies that have been stress-tested with the various oversight and tax experts in which a qualified FSP can claim expertise or to have access to expertise.

For our purposes here, we are going to call them buckets. A bucket is a strategy with which our students are knowledgeable enough to recommend as an option.

Some buckets, like customized versions of life insurance or managed accounts, may be ones the FSP can also implement as the stated expert. Others, like pension plans or ESOPs (Employee Stock Ownership Programs), may require an introduction to an ERISA-trained actuary and administrator.

The Decision Process software carefully vets and compares these concepts before we consider illustrating them for a client.

Since many FSPs are focused on clients whose primary concerns are *minimizing taxes and maximizing spendable income*, they are sometimes familiar with one or more of our buckets, or strategies if you prefer. That's because the options are few.

Life insurance–based wealth strategies are on the short list of many specialists, a fact often overlooked by those FSPs who do not have an insurance background.

The reader considering attending one of our events should know that life insurance is smack-dab in the wheelhouse of our education programs and is usually on our bucket list.

That fact is more a product of our commitment to objectivity than it is of our well-known insurance background. Given this, we believe life insurance should be included in the repertoire of any FSP presenting himself or herself as objective.

Our strategies are anything but buckets in the mind of the client, but we don't want to confuse our examples for informational purposes—with the detailed proposals the experts implement—with the appropriate prospect. That role is for others who are more qualified to give tax and financial advice, some of whom are part of our faculty at FSN.

What does all this mean for you?

If you're our kind of FSP, just as was the case with the needs-based salesperson of half a century ago, you will realize you are not in the product business.

> *We are in the business of helping prospects identify specific problems and make informed decisions, one problem at a time, but with several "buckets" to choose from. The rest is for another day or, perhaps, another adviser.*

Of course, the FSP will influence the decision with his or her expert opinions and valuable background narrative on each strategy. Again, that's what the prospect has paid you a fee for.

If the prospect needs more information, it should be provided by the FSP or, if need be, by the implementation specialist the FSP introduces for a given solution. Obviously, if helpful to the process, the other buckets considered in the evaluation process should be available to the prospect. It soon becomes apparent to the prospect that they have everything they need to make an informed decision.

Let's pause for a minute and think about how you and the prospect came to this conclusion. The selection of a strategy, a concept, or whatever solution chosen was a conclusion drawn at the end of a process, a process driven by a fully engaged prospect. Our favorite word, *perspective*, comes to mind.

From the prospect's *perspective*, something has happened that may only be realized subliminally, but it will be realized. They feel this is their choice, not yours or anyone else's. *It's their idea!*

How do we know?

Most prospects in our market are used to being pitched on a lot of investments. They are accustomed to our competition approaching them with *"an idea I'd like to share with you."*

That's as top-down and linear as it gets! Yet this is the approach a lot of financial advisers take with prospects and existing clients alike.

Although your prospects may not consciously recognize this stark contrast, their behavior will demonstrate their appreciation of your approach.

How do we know?

It's a dynamic process because the prospect is engaged the entire time. Not with lines we're hoping they will know, but with values, feelings, and concerns they may not even know they had, at least not relative to the issues you are discussing with them.

Like our discovery interview, the decision interview will be open-ended. No one knows for sure how it will turn out.

What we do know is that the FSP is not the boss. Nor is the prospect the boss. The situation (i.e., the problem) is the boss!

If your menu of alternative strategies contains some combination that works for the client, then the client will likely move ahead with you. Not because you show them the solution to their problem, but because they will help to create the solution themselves and have complete trust in your competence to execute it on their behalf.

> *As the FSP, or their internal, slices and dices the various scenarios, the software enables them to see the impact of those choices. You're pulling the levers on their behalf, with the understanding that how you arrived at a specific conclusion will be shared with the prospect.*[4]

If you've done your job correctly up to this point, the client has already decided to do business with you. The only question now is how they want to proceed. The adviser still maintains control of the process, but not as the sole decision maker. That's why we call it the Decision Process!

Again, our goal at this stage is to be accurate regarding the impact of a strategy. If the prospect wants to proceed with the appropriate expert, he or she will still get an illustration that is ultimately accurate, but unlikely to ever be precise, because most of the outcome depends upon future results that are not knowable.

That is why we should make it clear to prospects that we don't want to overpromise anything, especially the future. The only thing we can predict with certainty is that no financial product will perform exactly as illustrated.

> *We strongly advise against taking on the liability of showing best estimates that could be misunderstood as promises. If you show several scenarios, including the worst case, and explain them as such, it will be the strategy itself that causes the prospect to proceed.*

---

[4] *Note:* Advising, endorsing, or promoting any specific strategy is not the purview of this guide or of FSN.

We suggest that qualified FSPs use the Decision Process software to show two or more strategies that they are comfortable recommending to qualified prospects for their consideration.

If the strategies are presented properly, this technique will give the prospect the necessary breathing room to work though the alternatives and make an informed decision. Your fee helps to ensure that if they proceed, it will be with you. It also facilitates making a decision for reasons that should be apparent by now.

We must again emphasize that collecting a fee at the discovery stage is essential.

> *The culture we are progressing toward is one where you may not be compensated for selling products but for identifying agreed-upon problems and suggesting strategies and concepts that facilitate possible solutions—and then paid accordingly.*
>
> *Who can argue with that?*

Now let's look at the overall flow of the FSN Client Acquisition Process and see if we can tie everything together.

Rao-ism #15

If they were to remove the guardrails from bridges, how fast would you drive?

Authors' Note: We are the music teachers. The lyrics are the realm of others.

The adviser's operating platform, and that of other qualified experts provided by the FSP, including the IMO, CPA, or lawyer and broker dealer, is the source for specific illustrations and recommendations.

Our examples are for the purpose of showing how our software operates and how theoretical strategies could impact a client's cash flow, retirement, estate, or other finances. The funding and the use of specific products or product providers is not within our purview.

In our sales training, specific proposals are inserted as "placeholders" and are not to be presented or referenced in any way as indications of future results with clients or prospects. The numbers and assumptions are approximations and are only used to show how the software interacts with other variables and how changes impact the client's overall situation.

We are educators and trainers of salespeople with regard to the human element, not the firm element!

A Sales Process for the Ages

Thinking outside the box can not only be fun, it is sometimes necessary for survival. That is what survival training is all about. It disrupts our inner programing, the mentality of going through life on "auto-pilot," so that we can readily see bright new possibilities heading our way.

—Gail Pursell Elliott

AT THE start of this guide we stated that the authors are not likely to pass your way again. That may be a bit maudlin, as we expect to be around for a while. Whether we are or not, this guide is about you being around, rather than us.

We hope we have made a good case for the following:

Blending the lessons of the past with our more recent personal experience and examining the current realities we all face to chart a course for our future.

Here we're talking about a future that can be full of opportunity if you have the benefit of mentors and peers who share your values. We know what being alert to our changing environment, listening to our mentors, and joining study groups has meant to us.

If that sounds like we are recruiting the reader to join FSN, we plead guilty.

Like everything we have done over our careers, we wouldn't be involved if we didn't believe in it and in the value it brings to our students and FSN members.

If we're not the outfit for you, we encourage you to find at least one advanced market and forward-thinking organization to participate in. It may be a study group, a sales organization, or just one or more coaches or mentors willing to take you on. We sincerely mean that.

We are not the only resource for education and training. The others mentioned in this guide have earned excellent reputations and have made significant contributions to our industry. The important thing is to seek out mentors and a marketing platform that can give you an advantage going forward.

We believe the next few years can mark the beginning of a new golden age for independent FSPs who offer their services on a personalized basis. We are not happy, however, with the dearth of qualified talent waiting in the wings behind us.

> *For anyone under fifty, that spells enormous opportunity. They can go in any direction they wish, and FSN has the GPS.*
>
> *For anyone over fifty, it also spells enormous opportunity. Nothing is more exhilarating than reinventing yourself! We know that from firsthand experience.*

We must again state that to realize the potential these dynamic times hold, we all are going to have to adapt. That won't be easy, and it's not for everyone.

Our students are the best salespeople in the world. Most can and will do what it takes to adapt. We believe for them, and for us as well, that *the best years of our careers lie ahead of us!*

> *Now, the illustration that ties everything we've been discussing together:*

The two following diagrams illustrate the contrast between the sales approach that leads to irrelevance and the FSN Client Acquisition Process, which leads to indispensability.

First is the approach many FSPs have morphed into over the past three decades.

Second is the FSN Client Acquisition Process, for those FSPs wishing to adapt.

For some readers, we may be turning their sales process upside down!

> *This is the most important result of our journey over five decades of experience.*

"Quarterback"

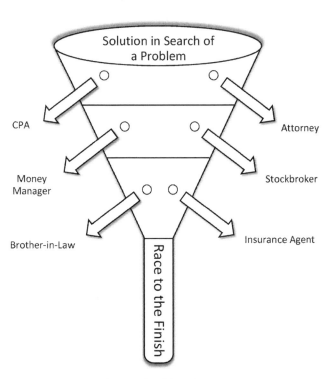

Solution in Search of
a Problem

CPA

Attorney

Money
Manager

Stockbroker

Brother-in-Law

Insurance Agent

Race to the Finish

Customized Versions
of a Single Strategy

Values Based Specialist
and Engaged Prospect

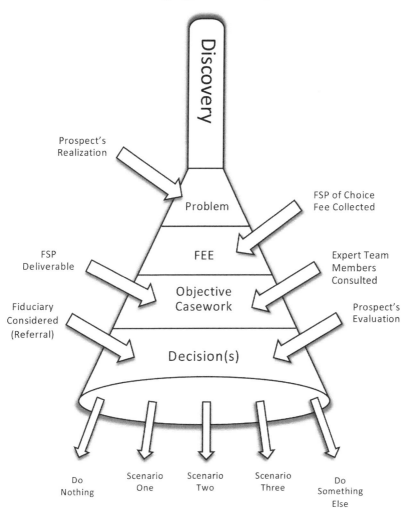

In our model, the prospect is paying for what you are about to show them, and hopefully paying well.

Why would any recommendation worth paying for not allow the FSP and/or the prospect to consider choices and even tweak the variables before the latter makes such a significant decision?

Well, most don't, and that's why we built our FSN Decision Process software.

There is a lot of problem-solving software out there, and we use some of it. What has always been missing is something that is solution agnostic.

Spreadsheets have attempted this for decades, but since the assumptions for each illustration are different (and they always are), comparing output is often meaningless.

After a lot of thought, we came to an obvious but often overlooked conclusion:

> *The dominant driver in most financial proposals is the assumed rate of return.*

We further concluded that the determination of that rate should be what the prospect feels is reasonable, not what the vendor competing for their business feels is possible!

Instead of one concept assuming one rate and a different concept projecting another one, how about leveling the playing field?

Here's our question:

> *If yield is one of the main drivers of most illustrations, how can a prospect make an informed decision between proposals when each one uses different yield assumptions?*

We're not just talking about an absolute interest rate here

either. We must also consider various costs and features of the proposal that are paid for out of the gross yield.

For example, if life insurance is used, mortality charges are a cost. If the need for a death benefit is not properly established, that can create misunderstanding.

On the other hand, taxes are often a primary consideration.

Our approach allows the FSP, or the prospect, to carry the yield (interest rate) of the choice from bucket to bucket and then to look at the other features and benefits of each plan without having their costs buried in the proposal.

The big aha here is that this approach gets the prospect away from thinking about the product performance and gets him or her focused on the strategy. The product(s) and illustrations are just the suggested means for funding the chosen strategy.

Of course, to make meaningful recommendations, we must also address things like risk tolerance, suitability, need for insurance, best interests, and other bites of information that vary from one FSP operating platform to another. Thus, even with this innovative tool, these things are matters of the FSP's best practices and, of course, of the oversight of compliance and governance under which she operates.

Our software facilitates these circumstances without overreaching our bounds. As a result, we keep it very simple:

> *Providing a measurement tool in addition to a proposal tool, our job is to show the impact of changing variables on different strategies, rather than to emphasize the performance of a given investment or product.*

The ultimate objective of most buckets in the Decision Process is to do these things:

> ➤ **Accumulate assets with minimum risk and minimum taxation in mind.**
> ➤ **Distribute assets with minimum risk and maximum spendable income in mind.**

This means that with most buckets, the two key drivers having to do with the numbers side of the equation are taxes and assumed yield. The rest is either valuable features and benefits and/or fluff and window dressing. Of course, these also must be included in any fair comparison, but they should be identified and weighed separately.

We usually assume that the asset component of a strategy is a constant. In the case of accumulation strategies, that means the same deposit or premium. We also assume a level annual disposable income with distribution strategies.

Other variables, such as age, health, and duration, are also important, but these are usually constants when designing a case. How they impact the result is another matter.

Then there are the values-based considerations that must also be included in any fair comparison.

For example, if a defined benefit pension plan is being considered, we must consider the requirement of including employees and paying administration fees. Will this create too much of a drag on performance for an acceptable result to be achieved?

Well, that depends on the cost, so we compare a defined benefit plan with and without these expenses.

Also, there are the subjective issues, such as the value the prospect places on employees and their retention.

Here's our routine question for the prospect regarding yield:

"Given your stated risk tolerance, if we come up with a

strategy that solves the problem we have identified, can you give us a benchmark yield that you would be comfortable assuming?"

The second thing missing from every other software offering we are aware of is *the global effect of a given strategy*.

Before a prospect agrees to go forward, they should be able to see how that decision impacts their overall cash flow. That's because the money they put with us doesn't come out of thin air. They must divert it from something else that it is currently being used for. The proposed strategy should be reinforced by the decision to rechannel these funds. If we can show that to be the case, the decision to move forward may become self-evident.

For example, in a split-dollar plan, the prospect may be borrowing money from their company to fund a key employee supplemental retirement plan. The money may be sitting in the company bank account at 1 percent to meet capital requirements or bonding minimums.

Now we may show it earning perhaps 6 percent, while still staying on the customer's balance sheet as a certified receivable—tax deferred! This is possible because of a proprietary bucket using split-dollar life insurance.

> *Being able to illustrate this source for the premium and using this kind of leverage can be a huge factor in a prospect's decision to move forward.*

In another example, we may fund the strategy from the cash flow of the business. That becomes quite a different matter.

A common concern of business owners is that there's no place they can achieve net gains on their capital better than by putting it back into the business they have built. They know and trust exactly what's being done with those funds! We may counter that argument with our Decision Process illustration of the "all your eggs in one basket" problem.

When life insurance is involved, we sometimes suggest the client consider premium financing. In these instances, things can get more complicated, but the Decision Process can sort them out and give the client a clear path to an informed decision—a path they will not easily find elsewhere.

The Decision Process Output and How We Present It

First, those who use our Decision Process software must concede a dramatic departure from much of what they've been taught about illustrating a client proposal.

Of course, your illustrations and proposals will ultimately be reasonably accurate using the products and underwriting of the FSP's choice and under the governance of their distribution platform.

Here's the rub: FSN doesn't provide a product-specific proposal for members using our Client Acquisition Process. That's up to the FSP or the specialist who is on their internal team, or a qualified associate with FSN. The tailor-made version of what the client bought into that you eventually provide through your operating platform is up to you.

To explain our position, we must again return to medicine. To be honest, the medical profession may be the archetype for our future!

Our final doctor analogy should sound very familiar:

After the diagnostics are completed, the doctor meets with the patient and explains his prognosis by using charts and diagrams of the human anatomy. If a surgical remedy is necessary, the doctor shows a diagram of the proposed procedure and course of treatment. Although this does not illustrate the client's specific anatomy, it will include his test results, x-rays, and the like, which give an accurate picture of the problem and illuminate the proposed solution.

> *The specific results can only be revealed by the execution of the strategy.*

In many cases there are choices offered to the patient that are based upon factors including risks, short-term discomfort leading to a long-term pleasing result and, of course, costs.

Naturally, patients may choose to do nothing or to go somewhere else. However, if *competence and trust* have been established, treatment based upon the current information the doctor has uncovered and the problem he has diagnosed is likely to move forward without interruption.

Sound familiar?

Our sale is with the problem and the remedial process to correct it. It is not with the spreadsheets or illustrations of specific products that imply results that cannot be guaranteed!

If all of this setup for the FSN Decision Process software seems excessive, it may be another example of the authors' propensity to overcommunicate.

We feel complete clarity is necessary for the genuine practice of objectivity and best interest, which is at the center of our Client Acquisition Process.

We provide the showroom versions of what the client buys into. Our numbers come from cutting-edge financial products and time-tested scenarios, but they are intentionally conservative.

> *We round our numbers down for simplicity and credibility, often as much as 10 percent less than the product providers suggest.*

Then, through their respective operating platforms, our members deliver a tailor-made finished product. And, of course, just as with a suit of clothes, the tailor doesn't go to work without the customer having some skin in the game. In our case this involves the payment of a fee.

We know what we are asking of our students.

For some, it's just not a practical option. For others, it's a compelling challenge. For still others, it will simply be a formal version of a path they have already chosen.

For those who buy in, our system is a road map (we prefer the term GPS) to indispensability in an industry that is surrendering our relevance to alternative resources—alternatives that we believe do not properly consider the client's values.

Here's our question:

Are any veterans of our business surprised that the financial institutions are greeting an alternative to manual distribution of their products with open arms?

> *Tough love from the last of a generation that still loves those who sell for a living!*

How the FSN Decision Process software works

Let's look at three prospects. All three are age 50, Male Non-Smokers, Preferred. Each has a net taxable income of $250,000.

From our initial interview, we learn that all three are receptive to a supplemental retirement plan of one type or another.

They are all married with children and have agreed to a need for life insurance. Note: Recognizing a need for life insurance is one element of discovery that, if downplayed, may diminish the value of the software.

Thorough fact finding reveals these details:

> **Prospect #1** is employed as a systems analyst and advanced programmer by a Fortune 500 corporation. He is a cog in the machinery and happy to remain valued but somewhat anonymous. He receives an annual bonus that is usually $40,000-$50,000, which is available for funding supplemental retirement.

> **Prospect #2** is self-employed. He owns a C corporation that controls an auto repair shop and three car washes. He is concerned about a secure retirement and would like to consider any tax advantaged way of setting up a disciplined program. He is willing to put up to $50,000 per year into a private or corporate retirement plan.

> **Prospect # 3** is employed by a large Government contractor. He receives annual bonuses that vary based upon the profits above the bidding prices that won the contracts for his employer. His bonuses are based upon things he doesn't control, but they are usually at least $50,000, which he agrees is available for funding.

The Decision Process software presents all examples for each prospect *with a single input of data.* It then contrasts, compares and offers detailed drill down on each strategy.

The software can correlate and present as many examples of different strategies as we wish. We also have many more sophisticated presentations that can be customized to prospects for things such as ESOPs (Employee Stock Ownership Plan), Pooled Income Funds, Charitable Trust, etc.

We have found considering five options to be the ideal presentation format. In reality, we are only offering three strategies, because two of the options we always suggest putting on the table are:

Option One: Do nothing and let the chips fall where they may.

Option Five: Go somewhere else and keep your fingers crossed.

Below, we will mention the other three possible strategies for each of our three prospects and give some specifics on the one that, based upon what we have learned, we decide to recommend.

We always provide a simple one-page overview, which can be formatted to the liking of the FSP. Caution; research shows that "artsy" or vendor provided presentation formats evoke skepticism from prospects.

The software then provides detailed drill downs to show where every number came from and the basis of every assumption. Yet, the single page for each option considered is the key to the prospect moving forward.

The numbers below are close to the final product, but rounded down by 5-10% for simplicity, as well as our commitment to being conservative.

As you look at these numbers, ask yourself: "Would 10% more or less make a difference to the prospect in deciding to proceed with a strategy?"

For our first prospect we generate illustrations of:

> ➤ A conservative mutual fund and a 20-year level term policy

➢ A Variable Annuity
➢ An Indexed Universal Life policy

After explaining all three options, we recommend a good accumulation IUL policy. A completely private transaction with no leverage, no obligations and relatively little risk.

Here's the summary of our one-page overview:

Earn $45,000 Gross. Pay State taxes (5%) and Federal taxes (35%) = $18,000

Net premium **$27,000** paid for 20 years until age 70

Cumulative outlay over twenty years: **$540,000**

Illustrated spendable income from age 70 to age-100: **$70,000** per year

Cumulative spendable income to client over thirty years: **$2,100,000**

Average death benefit from 50-100: **$600,000**

For our second prospect we generate illustrations of:

➢ A 401(k) plan
➢ A Defined Benefit Pension Plan
➢ Split Dollar life insurance using a quality IUL policy

After reviewing each option, we recommend the Split Dollar approach. No direct IRS involvement. No loopholes or interpretations of The Code. No employee participation. Just a venerable concept that is ideal for a C corp.

Here's a summary of our one-page overview:

The Split Dollar arrangement would be between the prospects' C corporation and the owner/employee (the prospect).

The result is a semi-private transaction using the arbitrage between the tax rates of the clients C corporation and his personal rate.

Earn $45,000 gross to the C corp. Since his state has no corporate income tax and the Federal tax rate is 21%:

Pay C corp. taxes $9,500

Net premium **$35,500**

is loaned to the owner/client each year and repaid to the C corp. at age 70.

Client pays interest only on the loan at the Applicable Federal Rate, or AFR.

Estimated cumulative interest paid (out of pocket) over 20 years **$100,000**

Cumulative premium and interest payments: **$810,000**

Illustrated annual spendable income from age 70 to age 100: **$86,000**

Cumulative spendable income over thirty years: **$2,580,000**, plus loan paid back to corporation of **$675,000** from cash value of IUL policy*.

*Total paid to client/owner over thirty years: **$3,255,000**

Average death benefit from age 50-100: **$500,000**

For our third prospect we generate illustrations of:

➢ A Fixed Indexed Annuity
➢ A Whole Life policy
➢ An IUL policy using partial premium financing

We review each choice, but suggest the IUL policy, using leverage provided by premium financing because of the projected superior performance.

The portion of the premium financed will come from a bank to offset taxes paid on the bonus.

Here is a summary of our one-page overview:

Earn $45,000

Pay State (5%) and Federal tax (30%) of $18,000

balance **$27,000**

Barrow **$18,000** each year from bank (approved premium finance provider)

Loan to be paid back at age 70 out of policy cash surrender value.

Net premium **$45,000**

Annual out of pocket: $27,000 + average annual loan interest of $1,750 = **$28,750**

Cumulative total outlay of premiums and interest over twenty years: **$575,000**

$360,000 Loan repaid to bank out of policy cash surrender value at age 70

Illustrated spendable annual income from age 70 to age 100: **$100,000**

Cumulative spendable income over thirty years **$3,000,000**

Average death benefit from age 50-100 **$850,000**

Although the input variables for our three prospects are identical, the results produced vary significantly based upon the strategy chosen.

Three Strategies	Average Death Benefit:	Cumulative Spendable Income to age 100
Prospect #1	$600,000	$2,100,000
Prospect #2	$500,000	$3,255,000
Prospect #3	$850,000	$3,000,000

The Rest of the Story

At first blush, the favored solution may work very well for each of our three prospects. Showing comparisons of two or more other concepts also facilitates a sound decision. Especially, if the other concepts are ones the prospect is more familiar with.

For example, they know what a mutual fund or a 401(k) is, but they probably don't know what Split Dollar life insurance is. How good is our recommendation? Compared to what? The Decision Process software answers that question.

Another reason for choices is because, no matter how much we emphasize it, many *FSPs simply don't do a thorough enough job with discovery.*

One reason: sometimes, when we have a great looking prospect, we hesitate to do thorough discovery because we don't want to hear about any deal killers!

We understand. That's the inherent optimism of sales people. But in this case, what you don't know can hurt both the prospect and you.

Let's play devil's advocate and look at our thee prospects again.

What if, we proceeded to the "close", only to learn in the process that:

Prospect #1, who we steered toward an IUL policy, received a DUI three months ago.

We didn't ask "is there anything that may affect your ability to qualify for life insurance? Anything physical, financial, or from a legal standpoint?"

Prospect #2, who we encouraged toward Spit Dollar, is planning to divorce his wife and has been advised to offer her 50% of all future earnings in his C corporation as part of the settlement.

We didn't ask the tough questions about his family situation. For example; "Will you want your wife to be involved with the process we are going to be working on?" Or, one of our favorites: "Is your current wife the mother of your children?"

Prospect #3, to whom we introduced a partial financed premium to leverage the potential result, has an aversion to debt. In fact, he has never allowed any credit card debt to carry beyond one month.

We didn't ask the simple question: "How does your overall

balance sheet look in regard to your assets relative to your liabilities?"

Here's our rhetorical question for you:

Since no client acquisition process can avoid dealing with these kinds of issues, when would you like to have found them out? Sooner or later?

From the standpoint of objectivity and the best interest rule, the Decision Process software is an ideal tool. Yet, without proper use of the Discovery Process, it is of little value.

The Process Is Your Product!

"I've got a guy."

FSN is a unique resource because dealing with the above kinds of cases is what we do. Puzzles like these are one of the things that our members cannot easily get help with elsewhere. Between our highly qualified members and our permanent faculty, we offer a menu of experts to respond to most prospects needs and opportunities.

Without the FSN Client Acquisition Process, we might have walked away from all three of the above situations and never known why we didn't win a new client. Without the FSN Decision Process software, we probably wouldn't have a fallback position.

With the Client Acquisition Process, even if we must walk away without a client, it will be without regret.

Indeed, it will be with the gift of confidence that only a professional process can give us.

Rao-ism #47

Of all my journeys, the longest was that from my head to my heart.

11

What Now? Suggestions on Adapting

Anyone offering financial advice that is doing business five years from today, the same way they are doing business today, will be out of business.

—Jerry Vanderzanden, CLU, ChFC,
noted industry expert and adviser to the authors

THE ONLY thing we aren't certain about regarding the above statement is the time frame. It could be more, it could be less.

With that in mind, we have tried in this guide to help the reader move to the high ground. Not for safety, but for a perspective from which to catch a glimpse of the future, a future in which we hope you discover ways to better serve clients.

As FSPs, no matter what type, our first duty is to *make sure the journey we chart for our client's financial success is a safe one.*

As teachers and mentors, we feel the same duty toward our students. We hope that some of our members receive and implement our counsel with the same kind of trust their clients place in them.

That said, *we cannot, nor would we, take on the same*

fiduciary responsibility *for our clients' safety that our readers do for some of their clients.*

You may have noticed that this is the first time we have dropped the f-bomb in the text of this guide. That's not by accident. Nor is it to diminish the importance of the word. On the contrary, *fiduciary* may soon become the biggest word in our lexicon. For now, it's a bit of a moving target. That said, the direction is clear!

As of this writing, the Fifth Circuit Court issued a ruling that vacates the Department of Labor's (DOL) authority regarding the fiduciary rule.

Before anyone feels relieved, the ruling had nothing to do with the soundness of the idea that there be a fiduciary rule governing the activities of FSPs. Rather, it points out that the DOL is an enforcement agency with no authority to draft or originate laws or rules.

What this ruling really means is very important to FSPs.

The fiduciary rule has clearly established agreement throughout the industry that the public is entitled to an expectation of objectivity and best interests from their FSP.

That bell cannot be un-rung by the courts. Instead, it will most certainly be reinforced by more than one regulatory authority with the power to enforce it.

Our belief is that the 2018 ruling has only made compliance with the spirit and intent of the fiduciary rule more important than ever. The only thing that concerns us now is, who's the appropriate enforcement agency?

Given these developments, it is also a subject upon which others are more qualified to speak. So, we're going to take the same approach we suggest the FSP take on behalf of their prospects and go to the best resource we know of on this subject. In market conduct and sales practices from the FSP's perspective, that would be our longtime partner and trusted resource Jerry Vanderzanden.

As one of the industry's most knowledgeable professionals on the subject, Jerry explains his view of the changing environment from the perspective of a former financial planner and fellow marketer.

Here are his thoughts. *Note:* Words in parentheses are the authors.

The Future for Advisers in a Fiduciary World

Operating as a fiduciary was the law of the land from June 2017, thanks to the Department of Labor. The DOL ruled that the FSP is a fiduciary where ERISA plans and IRAs are involved and must meet "impartial conduct standards." There can be no misleading statements, and you may accept only reasonable compensation on this class of business under the rule at that time.

The recent court ruling that vacated the DOL fiduciary rule has only energized various jurisdictions. Several insurance departments, mostly in progressive states, as well as the SEC, plan to reclaim their authority and regain the momentum of the DOL to increase and extend fiduciary or "best interest" responsibilities to all forms of FSPs.

Insurance companies, broker dealers, and regulators had already retooled their messaging, training, and supervision with the assumption that the fiduciary rule would be here to stay. In doing so, they have assured us that it still is.

The difference is that the responsibility for revising the existing rule is now fragmented. That likely means that RIAs (registered investment advisors) and IRAs (investment advisor representatives), broker-dealers and registered representatives, insurance marketing organizations, and insurance-focused practitioners will all be subject to some version of the Department of Labor fiduciary rule, where most transactions will require a *best-interest standard* if not a contract. We believe this may mean that very few financial transactions will be viewed as exempt from a best-interest standard. We are not certain if disgruntled clients will be forced to continue to use arbitration or will gain the right to sue in court as the DOL fiduciary rule would have ultimately allowed.

What is sure to follow will be a contest among those who oversee our industry to write the definitive rules governing the fiduciary role in our profession.

(One could say that what we have is one gorilla in the SEC and up to fifty monkeys in the state insurance departments, each drafting its definition of what being a fiduciary in our industry means.)

The prevailing belief among industry pundits is this: *No one believes the states will compete with one another based on the leniency of their approach! So, hang on and know that the fiduciary rule is alive, well, and growing tentacles.*

We should also note that clients, especially business owners and others with outside counsel, are generally aware of the DOL fiduciary rule. The truth is the public has received enough evidence over the past two years to justify assuming that any FSP they deal with is obligated to operate under the fiduciary rule.

Add to that the difficulty of explaining that we were only expected to observe the requirements of the fiduciary rule with qualified money but not with the other advice we render. That's called "conditional morality"—not something any of us want to be accused of.

There is no going back. We assume clients are going to expect a best-interest standard to apply to all interactions with financial advisers. They don't know or care about the fine print, which might limit the fiduciary definitions to only certain transactions.

One thing we can expect in coming years is that the industry will need to respond with more fee-based products to replace commission-based products as the clear bias against commissions deepens. This will have a dramatic impact on all forms of money-based products, such as annuities and securities.

For now, we don't expect any attempts to eliminate commissions as we know them from risk-oriented products such as life and disability insurance, critical illness, and long-term care. Over time, though, that too could change.

Other developed countries, for example, the United Kingdom and Australia, made even more sweeping fiduciary changes years ago that virtually eliminated commissions on financial products. The evidence to date seems to indicate that access to quality financial advisers has been significantly limited as a result. Now, regulatory authorities in those jurisdictions are beginning to look at ways to reintroduce commissions in some situations. Still, there is no talk of eliminating the fiduciary nature of an adviser's relationship with a financial client.

At the same time, they have recently introduced regulations in Australia that take the "best interest" rule to a new level by requiring new "competency" documentation from all financial advisers. The new rules invoke mandatory training that tracks with the "four E's" that are the basis of the CFP curriculum: education, examination, experience, and ethics.

We certainly can't argue with any standards that increase the likelihood of a better result for clients. However, we are concerned about the accelerating rate of increased standards outrunning the supply line of qualified FSPs.

Where's the Opportunity?

Competition from larger firms offering advice (all wearing the same jersey) means success for the individual practitioner will depend upon the following things:

> ➢ changing from being a generalist to a specialist
> ➢ understanding that holistic financial planning is just table stakes

To stand out from the large, deep-pocketed institutions, advisers need to find their areas of focus (unique ability).

While new layers of compliance add complexity and costs, the good news is that technology has the potential for the savvy adviser to continue to reduce not just the costs of compliance, but also the costs of marketing, client acquisition, fulfillment, and service, as well as time-saving tools such as planning software.

One major hurdle that remains is getting new clients and differentiating yourself, given the shift from suitability to fiduciary, for more and more aspects of your practice. This is of special concern for those whose business model depends on commission-based products. There was a time when just being a comprehensive financial planner was a virtuous and safe profession when ethically practiced.

The result of all that lies ahead is not entirely certain. Not only is the savvy adviser likely to avoid being marginalized, but also one could argue there has never been a better time to be a sole practitioner!

The first step is to be on the right side of technology, using it as an ally rather than a threat, not only as a rainmaker for lead generation to grow a practice but also as a facilitator for offering genuine objective advice to the consumer.

Then there's the tremendous scale that technology can bring

to the individual adviser in areas like service, client communications, processing business, and rendering of compliant business practices.

That said, *none of these fortunate developments in technology will matter if the adviser is not successful in differentiating herself.*

The advisers who marshal these issues into a cohesive business model will own their destiny in our industry. Benchmarking studies have supported that advisers who are focused on a specialty and have learned how to harness technology to their advantage will not only succeed in the future but also may enjoy unpresented financial results and vocational fulfillment.

Conclusions

As we conclude this guide, we find it ironic that our value proposition to our students and members looks a lot like what we are suggesting FSPs do in their business model for their clients.

We have identified our unique ability: mentoring, training, and coaching FSPs. Within that specialty, we bring subspecialists to our readers and members, like Jerry Vanderzanden and our faculty at FSN.

Jerry's advice was given with complete objectivity, other than his awareness of the authors' overall values and practices. Yet his views offer stunning similarity to our advice regarding layering a specialization over the FSP's existing practice to build positive momentum for coming changes. This is the kind of objectivity we hope the FSN Client Acquisition Process will bring to the clients of our students and members.

Jerry's views on our future also reinforce the credo that has been ubiquitous throughout this guide: The Golden Rule.

Given Jerry's observations, we suggest that FSPs even kick it up a notch and think of it as the Golden Law.

We finish our journey to indispensability with one final look at how adapting the FSN Client Acquisition Process may impact FSPs' strategy for success.

In the future environment we see, FSPs must identify those few things that are essential to the financial success of prospects in their target market. Then they must determine which of those things they believe they can deliver more effectively than the competition.

Note that we don't say more efficiently, because the services of others may be less expensive than yours. Efficiency is important to us too, but our goal is that *no one will be more effective than our members in delivering value to their customer.*

Your Product Is the Process, Not the Solution!

Once you've identified the items, work on refining and perfecting your offerings, and keep working at it until you are at the top of the competitive pyramid. Then, you will become *both a specialist and indispensable.*

One more time, we must overcommunicate the importance of avoiding being a one-trick pony by offering different versions of the same solution to most prospects.

To make this point indelibly clear, it is our informed belief that *the solution-in-search-of-a-problem approach is on its way to being outlawed!*

In what way could that affect you? With the FSN Client Acquisition Process, probably not at all.

We feel the FSN Decision Process software can also be a big help in avoiding that pitfall.

For some of the concepts you propose, you may be considered a fiduciary. For others you may recommend a sub-specialist, like a pension actuary, who assumes the fiduciary role. With still other strategies, there may be no fiduciary role required. It's the job of the adviser to make the appropriate determinations. Be sure you consult your oversight authorities on this one.

In each area of specialization, there are several subcategories that an FSP can spend a lifetime learning about.

The first step is to be sure you know which end of the problem you want to be on. It's not only medicine that figured this out long ago. We have patent lawyers and plagiarism litigators. We have commercial architects and building code specialists. We have tax accountants and forensic audit specialists. The former may engage the latter on a specific project, but not until they *discover a problem* for which that expertise is needed. Today's FSPs should follow their example.

It sounds like an oxymoron but be a generalist within your chosen specialty. Decide the buckets on which you also want to be the expert of choice. Then, assemble a team for any needed drill-down in other buckets or for needed support.

> *Assemble a team of* your choosing, *not someone else's. That's part of what you collect a fee for. It will also be a reason for belonging to FSN or another organization that provides similar resources.*

That may sound narrow, but it's just the opposite. None of your competitors are likely to have the level of expertise FSPs can offer with our model. Choose the right specialty, assemble the right support, and you will have little competition.

As we have discussed, our prospects are approached routinely by qualified financial advisers with ideas and concepts that are worth considering. We assume some are even outstanding opportunities. The problem for the prospect is our old friend perspective.

"How good is your idea?" "Compared to what?" "Is it something I'd seek out if I knew about it? Or is it something I am learning about because you want to sell it?"

How does that kind of proposition stand up against a tool that allows the prospect to compare strategies objectively, based on a need they have identified?

They can see the effect of changing variables and assumptions ripple through the spreadsheets. They can watch the impact of a given change in interest rates, or any other variable, on one or more of the strategies being considered. They also have other choices, including doing nothing at all or going somewhere else.

What this means to you is that *you should never again get trapped into competing with the ideas of other advisers.*

Why do we say this?

One last lesson from the past: Thirty-five years ago, in their classic book on running a successful business, *In Search of Excellence,* authors Tom Peters and Robert Waterman coined a phrase about marketing that has become a credo for us:

> *"hit 'em where they ain't!"*

We have used the converse of that suggested tactic by telling FSPs the following:

> *Never compete center stage, in the spotlight, toe to toe with anyone.*

To do so is to agree to the other person's terms of engagement, and that means you're going to cede the advantage to them.

> *More important, you are not in a contest, and it's*
> *not about you winning.*

Do effective discovery. Listen, and allow your prospect to tell you how to make him a client. Then, determine if one or more of those concepts in which you are competent should be included in the Decision Process meeting. Use tools and resources that aren't available elsewhere, the most important of which is you!

Hit 'em where they ain't!

For the FSP who is a sole practitioner, here's the important takeaway:

The higher up you go in a socioeconomic market, the fewer things you can offer with the comfort that a potential fiduciary must have.

Your specialty includes understanding the appropriate concepts and strategies that may deal with the problem(s) you and your prospect have identified. Stay narrow but go deep.

Then, perhaps with the counsel of others within your firm, or within your study group, or from among the members of the Financial Services Network, decide which ideas you feel qualify for the prospect's consideration.

Once that choice is made, the role of the adviser will vary.

If one of the choices being considered requires a higher level of specialization, the FSP's job is to help identify the best resources he or she knows of.

If you introduce others to help with appropriate strategies, make sure they are on the same team as you: the prospect's team:

Our hope is that FSPs will have their own handpicked experts on the strategies that support their chosen specialty, experts whom they know, trust, and respect.

In the case of FSN, we have members who are pension

actuaries; money managers; estate planning, tax, and elder care attorneys; ESOP specialists; CPAs; split-dollar experts; and the like. All have had extensive experience with the strategies discussed in this guide. This is just one credible source for FSPs in considering who, if anyone, they are comfortable recommending to clients. It's your choice and no one else's, but it is one of the most important decisions for every FSN going forward.

This approach to building a practice may seem risky. Are we saying that, after all your work, you should collect an initial fee but then pass on the lucrative implementation of a sophisticated strategy to a subspecialist?

Yes, but that doesn't mean you cannot be compensated.

Remember you are a *problem specialist*. For example, if your specialty is tax-advantaged strategies for wealth accumulation and succession planning for business owners, you will want to know something about ESOPs. A candidate for an ESOP would be an example of when you introduce another specialist before taking the next step. In this case, the individual is also a fiduciary.

With FSN, this would likely lead to employing one of the basic tenets of our organization discussed in Chapter 5, *joint work*.

Remember our definition of joint work includes other FSPs from all corners of the industry, not just salespeople. Whether you are a member of FSN or have other resources, go to the best and most trustworthy sources on behalf of your clients.

Again, you are not the quarterback inviting or allowing less-qualified professionals to weigh in on your work. That will only nullify the crossover issues that got you to this point. Instead, you are bringing in *a specialist within your specialty.* Someone who does only one thing: *support the design, implementation, and oversight of strategies on your limited and specialized menu.*

In addition to joint work on any commissionable products involved, sharing fees is completely ethical, so long as there is full disclosure and it is conducted along the guidelines of your governing body or SRO (self-regulatory organization).

That, however, is not our recommended course of action.

In cases where we have brought in a specialist, such as an actuary, administrator, money manager, or tax attorney, the plan specialist does all the analytics, presentations, and drafting of documents and *receives all the fees* related to his or her work. We write all the life insurance that is deemed appropriate in the plan. Everyone is happy.

With or without the fiduciary rule, there is one last contradiction in terms we can pass along with certainty:

> *The more experienced you become, the fewer things you know for sure.*

How do we know?

When we were younger, our pat answer to every question from a prospect about the breadth of our knowledge on a particular need was the same: "Sure! We can do that!" Then we'd scramble to find out what we had promised. Today that would be a dangerous tactic!

We are reminded of the words of a mentor of ours who used to say something to us that we never quite understood at the time:

> *"I don't know much, but what I do know, I know better than anyone!"*

Another of our favorite phrases that needs to be converted into more compliant language is this: if you are not conversant enough on a given subject to answer the basic questions that come from a prospect, you should never hold yourself out to your prospect as a credible resource on that subject.

That said, let's be clear about things that fall under the aegis of your specialization.

These are things about which you are knowledgeable enough to have an intelligent discussion but for which you may not see yourself as the implementation source, especially if a fiduciary role is called for.

Select an operating platform or partner with a firm that has an appropriate team that is on call but only paid for as needed.

If you are an FSN member, we can provide much of what your prospects may need in the way of expertise on tax-advantaged strategies, even if it means suggesting they do something else or nothing at all.

> *That's something your prospects and clients cannot easily get elsewhere.*

Rao-ism #23

There are two very important days in your life: the day you are born and the day you discover why. Have you discovered your why?

Afterword: The Significance of Your Indispensability

In times of rapid change, standing still is the most dangerous course of action.

—Brian Tracy

WHAT YOU have just reviewed suggests a fundamental transition in the approach most FSPs take to selling financial strategies, services, and products.

If the FSN Client Acquisition Process was introduced for no other reason than the value it delivers to consumers, that would be reason enough for FSPs to buy in.

That said, the situation behind FSN's introducing our Client Acquisition Process is to offer students and members a proactive response to three industry dynamics, all moving in the same direction:

➤ The evolution of *the self-directed consumer*, facilitated by technology that has enabled access to unlimited information and advice, much of it for free.
➤ The *rush to eliminate the human element* from an inherently personal process, a process that belongs in the realm of legal, medical, and even psychiatric advice, as

opposed to being diminished by efficient, but less effective, automated alternatives.

> ➢ The progressive regulatory position that *the public is better served by a homogenized version of FSP*, whose counsel is uniformly available to all, under similar terms of engagement.

These statements are not intended to be disruptive, but the situation they portend is disruptive, so we must continue to adapt, while keeping the following in mind:

The situation is the boss!

We are counting on two truths, both based upon those things that never change. They are also two things that will be instrumental in helping financial advisers achieve indispensability.

First is our belief that *human behavior cannot be improved by legislation or regulation. It can only be punished or ignored.*

That may sound controversial, but from a governance standpoint, the FSP should be just as invisible to industry regulation as he or she is to the police or the FBI. In other words, they should be mindful of the rules and should never have occasion to meet, other than under routine circumstances.

If you were raised by the right parents, or taught by the right teachers or clergy, or subject to any moral imperatives growing up, you probably agree with us.

It all boils down to that one value woven throughout this guide: the golden rule.

Second is our belief that *technology is unable to detect the inflection in a prospect's voice or the messaging that is apparent between his or her spoken lines.*

After decades of enhancing our performance with electronic window dressing, our industry is now going down a slippery slope. We are programming machines to deliver problem-solving output by filling in the blanks, *using the machine's language, rather than that of the prospect.* In doing so, we miss the most important bits of information[5]—*the unspoken ones.*

These nuances are the things upon which the FSN Client Acquisition Process is based. It is a process that encourages discovery by the prospect of problems that may have more than one solution—perhaps even problems for which no solution exists, all presented with competence, trust, objectivity, and transparency.

> *Advisers who have the courage to occupy this space will achieve indispensability.*

At FSN, it is not our purpose to challenge our changing environment. Rather, *our unique ability* is to understand it, then to be innovative in how we train others to adapt to it. That's the behavioral changes we intend to influence. It is the thing that will make all of us indispensable to our customer.

That is a result no one can quarrel with.

---

[5] 1 Technology use for basic information gathering and fact finding with prospects is a wonderful tool. In our view, when technology crosses over into recommending strategies and solutions, it greatly exceeds its logical boundaries.

APPENDIX: WHAT IS THE FINANCIAL SERVICES NETWORK?

WE ARE a membership organization dedicated to educating, training, and mentoring the financial service professional (FSP), with an ongoing commitment to innovation. Members include financial advisers, RIAs, money managers, insurance agents, annuity specialists, bank retail planners, and financial planners. Associate members include CPAs, attorneys, and other nonretail FSPs.

Education

Our education programs revolve around the latest and most effective wealth strategies for business owners, the self-employed, and affluent seniors.

What makes us unique is that our faculty consists only of highly successful specialists who are dedicated to not only sharing their life's achievements but also mentoring our members on their respective career journeys. *This core benefit exists nowhere else that we are aware of.*

Our members learn from actual case studies and role-playing with the industry's best. They also have ready access to our faculty for coaching and guidance up to and including our wiliness to do joint work on a selective basis. This too is something we believe is not available elsewhere.

Training

Most would agree that over the past two decades, virtually all resources for training in the science and art of selling financial services have been supplanted by oversight, consumer protection, and defensive measures to shield the financial institutions from liability.

In the process, financial service professionals have been overloaded with precautionary measures and mountains of information, with virtually no industry resources being dedicated to their professional development and success. As a result, we have an industry of dedicated providers who are *on their own* when it comes to developing skills and talents for their chosen profession. This reality is the reason for the creation of the FSP legacy for our industry.

Mentoring

Over our long careers we have been blessed to be mentored by some of the legendary figures of our industry. We had the privilege of knowing and being guided by the example and works of the best of those who built our industry in the post–World War II era.

Later, we were fortunate enough to achieve prominence in our own right. Over the past decades we have had the opportunity to mentor and coach dozens of promising young professionals. To our delight, some have become the best of the best and carry on our tradition. Mentoring is our greatest legacy, and it is the primary reason for the establishment of FSN.

We have a library of knowledge that cannot be transferred

any other way than by one-on-one personal coaching. Above all, we are devoted to mentoring our members as a core value of FSP.

The FSN Client Acquisition Process (CAP) Is Your GPS to the Future

We believe that the product of today's financial services professionals is not the solutions they offer to clients, but rather *the process* by which they arrive at and present those solutions. Otherwise, we will eventually surrender our perceived value to technology and progressive views of the delivery system for our services.

To understand that statement is to understand *the very thing that makes us necessary to begin with.* The process, not the solution, is what can make the FSP indispensable to his or her clients.

Knowing what must occur to acquire a new client is only half the challenge. To be sure, success cannot occur without touching all the basis in the FSN CAP. Once we know WHAT needs to be done, it's the "how" we address the problem.

It's the "how" *of the solutions we provide that is our unique ability and the reason for our fee.*

We know the "how" because we have some of the best first-hand experience available. More importantly, we know how to teach the how! And we do it with no holdbacks! Nothing behind the curtain. No magic sauce that members must pay additional premiums for. Our members get everything we've got to give. We only ask that they complete our curriculum to become certified in our process. Above all, we ask that they *never* share the *how* without collecting a fee!

It is obvious by our many decades on the front line that we won't be passing this way again. That's why we want to formalize what we have to pass on through the creation of FSN. We are excited about our offering to the FSP community.

The FSN CAP is the foundation of our education and training. It is a proven successful process that we help our members master. CAP is founded on a set of circumstances that decades of experience has taught us must occur in harmony for a successful client relationship to occur.

It is not about selling but about *the flow of the client acquisition process itself.* A process that must ebb and connect, step by step, for the FSP to be sure that, in every case, he or she is doing the right things right!

When that happens, we have what we call; **No-regrets selling, meaning that if the client could have been acquired, they would have. No looking back or wondering whether you should have done things differently.**

There are six basic steps in the flow of the process, all of which are taught and drilled in detail at our FSN Summit events.

The Process Is Your Product!

> ➤ **Prospecting.** Getting in front of enough of the right kind of people under favorable conditions. Easily enough said. A moving target in today's high-tech world.
> ➤ **Opening cases.** This step is what we call "the selling heart," after a book written by one of our mentors over fifty years ago.
>> 1. Approach—Your value proposition to get an appointment.
>> 2. Discovery—Establishing competence and trust to uncover problems.
>> 3. Crossover—How to win an engagement and collect a fee.

- ➤ **Developing strategies.**
    1. Evaluate your discoveries and consider options.
    2. Consult your FSN team to make recommendations.
- ➤ **Decision Software.** A sophisticated calculator offering objective choices.
- ➤ **Presenting strategies.**
    1. Objectivity and prospect engagement in the process.
    2. Layered presentations (a one-pager on top of an encyclopedia).
    3. An informed decision made by the prospect.
- ➤ **Continuing the cycle with an ongoing prospecting and marketing strategy.**

FSN provides the most-qualified faculty in financial services to share their best practices regarding performing these six fundamental steps in the Client Acquisition Process.

Financial Services Network
Fsnprocess.com
800.997.5282

BIBLIOGRAPHY

Bachrach, Bill. *Values based selling*, Insight Publishing, 1989.

Letterman, Elmer G. The Sale Begins When the Customer Says No. Papamoa Publishing, 2017. First published under the same title in 1953.

Peters, Thomas J., and Robert H. Waterman. *In Search of Excellence.* New York: Harper & Row, 1988.

Rackham, Neil. *Spin Selling*, London, England, Random House, 1989.

Sullivan, Dan. *Your Unique Ability.* New York: McGraw-Hill, 1986.

Whiting, Percy H. *The Five Great Rules of Selling.* New York: McGraw-Hill, 1959.